Invest Smarter with AI: A Prompt-Driven Guide to Better Investing

Invest Smarter with AI:

A Prompt-Driven Guide to Better Investing

MARK A. JOHNSON PHD

Published by
Manage My Own Investments LLC
Email: info@managemyowninvestments.com

Hardcover ISBN: 979-8-9943118-2-0
Paperback ISBN: 979-8-9943118-0-6
eBook: 979-8-9943118-3-7
Audiobook: 979-8-9943118-1-3

First published in 2026
Printed in the United States of America

IMPORTANT DISCLOSURE

This book is provided for educational and informational purposes only. It is not intended to provide, and should not be construed as, investment, financial, tax, legal, or accounting advice. Nothing in this book constitutes a recommendation, solicitation, or offer to buy or sell any securities, financial products, or investment strategies.

The information and examples presented are general in nature and may not be appropriate for all individuals or situations. Financial decisions involve risk, including the potential loss of principal. Readers should consult with qualified professionals regarding their specific financial circumstances before making any investment or financial decisions.

While the author and publisher have made reasonable efforts to ensure the accuracy of the information contained in this book as of the date of publication, they make no representations or warranties regarding its completeness or continued accuracy and accept no liability for any losses arising directly or indirectly from the use of this material.

Dedication

"If I have seen further, it is by standing on the shoulders of giants."
—Isaac Newton

To my family—thank you for allowing me to stand on your shoulders.
I miss you, Dad.

ABOUT THE AUTHOR

Mark A. Johnson, PhD, is the faculty fellow in Investments and Portfolio Management and a teaching professor at Wake Forest University. He brings nearly two decades of experience as a finance professor and real estate investor, which includes over two years as a registered investment advisor. Born in New Orleans, Louisiana, Johnson is known for his ability to simplify complex financial concepts, which has earned him over twenty teaching and professional awards from institutions including Wake Forest University, Loyola University Maryland, and Florida State University.

His research interests include financial markets, investments, and financial literacy. He is a recipient of the Poets&Quants' Best 40 Under 40 honor as an educator and has published research in the field of personal finance. His insights have been featured in numerous outlets, including US News & World Report, Fortune, Bankrate, CNN Underscored Money, Yahoo Finance, MarketWatch, Business Monthly, HuffPost, and WalletHub. He regularly discusses market trends, investments, and personal finance topics in these publications.

Johnson frequently speaks with students, families, nonprofit organizations, athletes, and professional groups on the importance of financial literacy and making smarter financial decisions.

THE USUAL (ALBEIT IMPORTANT) DISCLAIMER

Before we dive in, a quick note: this book aims to teach and guide, not to provide personalized financial advice. I will walk you through examples and ideas that you can adapt to your own situation, but how you apply them will depend on your specific goals and circumstances.

The views shared in this book are my own and do not reflect those of my current or former employers. My goal is to help you gain confidence in managing your finances and investments, not to offer one-size-fits-all advice. Before making any major financial decisions, consider consulting with a qualified professional.

CONTENTS

PREFACE

Growing up, we were often taught that money was a private matter, and asking someone about their earnings, spending, or investments was considered rude or inappropriate. That silence, however, comes at a grave cost. In nearly two decades of teaching finance, I have seen how many people feel lost when it comes to managing their money. Sometimes, they are unsure of where to start and whom to trust, and they often feel overwhelmed by conflicting advice, buried in terminology and anxious about making the wrong financial decision.

At the same time, we live in a world that offers us more access to powerful financial tools than ever before. What used to require a spreadsheet, a phone call, a broker, and a lot of guesswork can now be done in minutes with your phone on an app. This is especially true with artificial intelligence (AI). AI is transforming many aspects of our lives, including how we analyze investments, track spending, plan for retirement, and make sense of an increasingly complex financial world.

However, if not used properly and wisely, technology can exacerbate poor decision-making. This book is not focused on turning you into a tech expert; rather, it is about providing you with a practical way to use AI to think more clearly and make smarter financial decisions. I believe that with the right guidance, you can leverage AI to improve your approach to financial life—not just the numbers, but also the trade-offs and decisions involved.

This book is for individuals who want to be more intentional with their money. It is for readers who want to learn about becoming better investors and how to utilize a now readily available tool—AI—to assist in this process. Regardless of whether you are new to investing or already doing many things right, my goal is to make the financial world feel less intimidating and demonstrate how AI can be a practical ally in this journey.

Let me stress this crucial point further: I am a finance professor and have spent years helping people understand how finance works in the real world. This book is meant to educate, not provide personalized financial advice. I will guide you through concepts and prompts that you can customize and use, but how you apply them will depend on your own situation.

INTRODUCTION

Although artificial intelligence (AI) cannot make your financial decisions for you, it can help you make smarter ones. AI can sift through mountains of information, clarify confusing concepts, and help you see your options more clearly. The real value of AI lies in its adaptability to your needs. Whether you are determining how much to save, how to invest based on your risk tolerance, or how to stay on track for retirement, AI can simplify the process. It does so by taking complex financial questions and breaking them down in a way that aligns with your goals, lifestyle, and pace. When used correctly, it brings clarity, structure, and momentum to your financial journey.

We are living in an era when advanced financial programs that once belonged to Wall Street are now in your pocket. AI can analyze your portfolio, identify risks, run projections, and guide you through significant financial trade-offs whenever needed. However, with all that power emerges a new challenge: you still have to lead. AI does not know your goals, your values, or what financial freedom means to you; that is your responsibility. Once you define those elements, AI becomes an incredible partner to assist you. This book is designed to demonstrate how to use AI to sharpen your financial acumen, maintain focus on what matters, and make decisions with greater confidence and less stress.

Why I Wrote This Book

I have spent nearly two decades as a finance professor teaching students how to think critically about money, markets, and finance as a discipline. Over the years, I have seen both the successes and the challenges people encounter while dealing with personal finance. Given the rise of AI, I wanted to create a resource that shows people how to use this new technology to make smarter financial decisions.

AI is only as effective as the prompts you provide (garbage in, garbage out). Therefore, I wrote this guide to show you how to use AI effectively for everything from budgeting and saving to portfolio construction and retirement planning. Regardless of whether you are an experienced do-it-yourself (DIY) investor, a beginner, or someone looking to make better financial decisions, this book offers processes to follow, prompts to try, and strategies to consider.

What Makes This Different?

This is not another investing book peddling generic advice, nor is it a technical manual. I am also not trying to convince you to trust a robot with your financial planning. Instead, I aim to show you how to combine your judgment with the power of AI to make better personal finance decisions.

You will still be the one setting your goals, choosing your trade-offs, and deciding how to act. However, AI can assist you in:
- running hypothetical scenarios and simulations you are curious about;
- checking for blind spots and biases in your thinking;
- modeling different outcomes instantly; and
- personalizing your financial strategy to fit your goals.

16

Today, AI is accessible to nearly everyone. The key is knowing how to use it effectively.

What This Book Covers

This book is designed to take you step-by-step through the financial planning process, illustrating where and how AI can assist along the way. Feel free to read it cover to cover or jump to the parts that matter most to you. Each chapter includes straightforward explanations, examples, and specific prompts you can use with AI platforms.

Let's walk through what each chapter covers so you know what to expect.

Chapter 1: How to Use This Guide

We begin with a quick overview of how to get the most out of this book. I will show you how to use the included AI prompts, how to effectively input information into an AI tool, and what to expect in terms of output. You do not need to be a tech expert as long as you are willing to experiment and refine your approach as you go.

Chapter 2: Making Good AI Prompts for Smarter Investing

The quality of your financial insights depends on the quality of your questions. This chapter teaches you how to write clear, specific, and context-rich prompts that yield meaningful results. It includes dozens of examples and tips for refining your approach as your goals evolve.

Chapter 3: Principles of Investing You Should Not (and Cannot) Automate

Some aspects of investing should not be outsourced to AI. This chapter discusses those elements and the timeless principles of investing that remain relevant, even in a world dominated by advanced technology.

Chapter 4: What Are Your Goals?

Financial planning is goal-driven. Whether your aim is retiring early, buying a home, saving for college, or simply achieving greater peace of mind, your goals shape everything to follow. In this chapter, we define clear, realistic, and motivating financial goals and use AI to map out what it takes to reach them.

Chapter 5: Current Financial Situation

Before you can build a plan, you must understand your starting point. This chapter guides you through how to gather and organize your income, expenses, debts, and assets, as well as how to use AI to create a personal financial statement.

Chapter 6: Risk and Risk Tolerance

Investing, fundamentally, is about managing trade-offs. Higher returns typically come with increased volatility. This chapter helps you understand your risk tolerance and how to construct a plan that aligns with your comfort level.

Chapter 7: Popular Investment Accounts and Asset Location

Not all investment accounts are taxed equally. We will examine various investment accounts, such as individual retirement accounts (IRAs), 401(k)s, and taxable accounts, and explain how to utilize each. You will also learn how to use AI to optimize asset location and withdrawal strategies.

Chapter 8: Assets to Own

We will explore the five major asset classes—stocks, bonds, cash, real estate, and alternatives—and how they work together. This chapter explains the role each plays in your portfolio (if any) and how AI can assist you in researching and monitoring your mix over time.

Chapter 9: What About Alternatives?

Cryptocurrency, real estate, private equity, venture capital, farmland, collectibles—you name it. This chapter simplifies alternative investments, explains who they are suitable for, and clarifies how to evaluate them with the help of AI. It also highlights the risks associated with chasing returns.

Chapter 10: Test Before You Invest

One of the most significant advantages of AI is its ability to help you simulate investment strategies before committing real money. This chapter demonstrates how to backtest a portfolio, forecast different scenarios, and stress-test your assumptions using AI prompts.

Chapter 11: Portfolio Construction with AI Help

Here, you will learn how to use AI to build a diversified, goal-aligned portfolio from scratch or adjust your current one. This includes guidance on asset allocation, rebalancing, tax efficiency, and staying within your risk limits.

Chapter 12: Rethinking Retirement

Retirement is the point at which work becomes optional. This chapter addresses key questions surrounding retirement planning, including how to use AI to determine which accounts to draw from in retirement, Roth conversions, and required minimum distributions (RMDs).

Chapter 13: Putting Everything Together

Now that you have assembled the pieces of your plan, it is time to see how they fit together. We will review how to create a financial plan using AI, how to revisit and update it regularly, and how to track progress without feeling overwhelmed.

Chapter 14: Let AI Be Your Second Set of Eyes

Most investment mistakes are avoidable and stem not from poor markets but from poor behavior. This chapter covers the most common financial missteps, such as panic selling, chasing performance, ignoring taxes, or allowing fees to pile up—and yes, we will cover how AI can help you catch yourself before going off track.

Chapter 15: Avoiding Common AI Investing Mistakes

AI is powerful, but it is not perfect. This chapter explains how investors can make costly mistakes if they are not careful when using AI to guide investment decisions. The chapter offers practical guidelines for getting the most out of AI while using it responsibly.

Final Thoughts

We will conclude by offering encouragement to keep going, asking questions, learning more about personal finance, and refining your plan. Financial planning is not a one-time task; it is a living, breathing process. Thanks to AI, you now have access to tools and insights to continue improving it over time.

Who This Book Is For

This book is for individuals who want to be thoughtful with their money and become better investors through lifelong learning. It is for the people who do not want to rely solely on experts but also do not wish to navigate everything on their own. Additionally, it is for investors who understand that money itself is not the goal but the means to becoming better with your finances and creating a life that truly matters to you.

If you have ever thought,
- "I do not know if I am doing enough financially,"
- "I wish I had someone to point out what I am missing,"
- "I want to understand this stuff without getting lost in the weeds," or
- "I paid for a financial plan, but I want a second opinion," then this book is for you.

I wrote this to be practical and helpful. I hope you enjoy it and use it to take real steps toward your goals. If you are ready to take the next step toward managing your finances with clarity and the help of AI, let's get started.

CHAPTER 1

HOW TO USE THIS GUIDE

"Tools are only as useful as the hands that wield them."
—Unknown

Investing can feel like learning a foreign language, especially when the speakers are talking quickly and throwing around acronyms. For most people, that is where the intimidation begins. Turn on any financial news channel, and you are bombarded with stock tickers running across the screen, analysts disagreeing, and charts that may be difficult to understand. It is easy to feel as though the world of investing was designed to confuse you.

Adding to this is the constant news cycle of headlines about potential recessions, interest rate changes, and overall economic uncertainty, which can easily lead to anxiety or second-guessing your finances. No wonder so many people either avoid investing altogether or make reactive, fear-based decisions. Even individuals with good intentions and decent incomes can feel stuck. They want to invest and know it matters, but they are overwhelmed by the options and unsure of whom or what to trust.

It does not help that many of us were raised to believe that money is a private matter—something not to be discussed at the dinner table, with friends, or even with family. This silence often leaves people unprepared and confused, feeling as though they are the only ones who do not have it all figured out. The truth is that discussing money openly and honestly is one of the best ways to learn and take control of your financial future. That is where AI—and this guide—enters the picture.

A New Tool for a New Era

If you have ever felt uncertain about how to invest, you are not alone. Just as spreadsheets transformed budgeting in the 1980s and index funds reshaped investing in the 1990s, we are now seeing AI influence the way people plan, allocate, and manage their money. Today, AI can accomplish in seconds what used to take hours. It can now analyze a portfolio, spot red flags, simplify complex concepts, or even suggest an investment mix that aligns with your goals and risk tolerance. Moreover, some tools can track your spending patterns, project your retirement income, or translate financial headlines into understandable language. While this does not mean you will never need to make a decision again, it does mean that you no longer have to navigate everything alone or in the dark.

I have witnessed firsthand how people struggle with financial decisions—not because they are unintelligent or disinterested, but because money is personal, and the tools we have traditionally used have not made it easier. That is rapidly changing. AI can level the playing field in a way we have not seen before, putting high-quality investing insights at everyone's fingertips to deliver analysis, comparisons, and explanations in seconds. It transforms what can be complex financial data for some into clear, actionable information faster than ever before. Thus, this guide shows you how to use AI to inform yourself and boost your confidence in making decisions.

What You'll Learn (And What You Won't)

This book is not a list of hot stock tips or get-rich-quick schemes. It will not tell you which fund to buy or how to "beat the market." Instead, it will teach you how to use AI to make smarter financial decisions for yourself. Below is what we will cover:

- What AI actually is and what it is not
- How AI can help you evaluate your current financial situation
- How to use AI to set better goals, define your risk tolerance, and build a diversified portfolio
- Where AI excels (such as crunching numbers and simulating outcomes)
- Where human judgment still matters (like defining your priorities, adhering to a plan, and making trade-offs)

Each chapter guides you through a key component of a solid financial plan and shows you precisely how AI can support that step. You will receive real-world examples, simple explanations, and AI prompts to modify and use for yourself. AI is no longer just for experts; it is for anyone with a smartphone and a willingness to learn. With the right prompt, you can ask AI to:

- analyze your portfolio's diversification,
- compare expense ratios on similar funds,
- project your retirement needs based on your savings rate,

- evaluate the impact of higher inflation on your budget, and
- suggest ways to rebalance without triggering significant tax bills.

And that is just the beginning!

The Limits of AI

There is a reason that ChatGPT's page states, "ChatGPT can make mistakes. Check important info." Evidently, AI is not perfect. It does not understand how you feel when the market drops 10% in a day, nor does it know your values, your past financial mistakes, or how you define "success." It will not remind you that your real goal is not to beat the market but to build the life you want.

AI also does not automatically make good decisions. If you ask vague or misleading questions, you will receive vague or misleading answers. That is why this guide emphasizes how to use AI. When used effectively, AI enhances your decision-making; however, if used incorrectly, it can accelerate mistakes. Chapter 15 provides tips on how to avoid errors when using AI.

What to Expect

This guide is designed to be hands-on, so feel free to jump around based on your needs and familiarity with investing. In most chapters, you will find (1) AI prompts you can customize and use and (2) mini case studies of a prompt in use, AI output received, and its interpretation. Regardless of whether you are just getting started, interested in building a financial plan, or revisiting your plan after years of investing, this book will help you gain a better understanding of what you want to accomplish and how AI can help you achieve it.

Quick Note

I am a finance professor, not your financial advisor, so I do not know your complete financial picture. Nothing in these pages should be considered specific financial, legal, or tax advice. The goal is to help you understand how to use AI as a resource, not to replace sound judgment or professional guidance when necessary.

This book was developed and tested using ChatGPT, one of the most accessible AI platforms available at the time of writing. The prompts and examples stem from my work with ChatGPT, but you can use them on other AI platforms such as Claude, Copilot, Gemini, or Perplexity, to name a few. Each may respond slightly differently, which can help you gain new perspectives. Different platforms may interpret prompts differently or offer varying levels of accuracy and depth. There are numerous AI tools available, and I encourage you to explore and find what works best for you. Please use this guide as a starting point to discover what is possible and always double-check your analysis or approach before making any financial decisions.

CHAPTER 2

MAKING GOOD AI PROMPTS FOR SMARTER INVESTING

*"Asking the right questions takes as much skill as giving
the right answers."*
—*Robert Half*

AI is a term that describes machines capable of mimicking certain types of human thinking. At its core, AI processes information, identifies patterns, and produces results—similar to how we make decisions. The difference is that AI can analyze vast volumes of data in seconds and continuously learn from new information without becoming tired or emotional. It is not magic; it is mathematics and statistics working at scale.

We have reached this point due to a perfect storm of technological advancements. Over the past couple of decades, we have witnessed significant increases in computing power, access to data, and improvements in machine learning algorithms, which have formed the foundation of AI. Tools like ChatGPT do not think like humans; they are trained on extensive amounts of text and data, and they have become adept at predicting what words, numbers, or ideas should follow based on previously observed patterns.

It Is All About the Prompt

When people ask me how to get the most out of AI tools like ChatGPT for investing, the first thing I tell them is that it is all about the prompt. The quality of what you receive depends on the quality of what you ask. Think of prompting like asking a research assistant for help. If you walk into a room and say, "Tell me the fastest way to get rich," you are unlikely to get a useful answer. The question is simply too broad. However, ask, "What are three low-cost ETFs[1] that I could use to build a globally diversified portfolio with a moderate risk profile?" and now we are talking. Learning how to communicate effectively with AI will help you get useful and personalized investment guidance without becoming overly technical.

AI is not a mind reader; it operates based on the information you provide. A good prompt offers enough detail to guide it in the right direction without overwhelming it. The better your input, the more useful your output. This principle applies whether you are seeking assistance to compare two funds, analyzing your portfolio, creating a savings plan, or stress-testing a retirement scenario. Learning how to write a good prompt is similar to learning how to ask the right question. In finance, that is often half the battle.

---

1   ETFs, or exchange-traded funds, are baskets of investments like stocks or bonds that you can buy and sell on an exchange, just like a regular stock. They're an easy way to get instant diversification without needing to pick individual companies.

Before you write anything, take a moment to ask yourself what you want to learn, decide, or create. A general prompt such as "Tell me about investing" will bring back general answers. When you ask for a specific type of help, such as a recommendation or an analysis, you will receive a response that is much more useful. Here are a few examples:

Weak Prompt
- "Tell me about ETFs."

Stronger Prompt
- "What are some low-cost ETFs that track the S&P 500, and how do they compare in terms of expense ratios and performance over the past 10 years?"

This stronger prompt transforms a general topic into something personal and decision-ready.

It is also beneficial to include relevant details. The more context you provide, the better AI can tailor recommendations to your risk tolerance, investment goals, time horizon, and constraints. You do not need to write a novel, but you should include the information you would share with a human financial advisor.

Key details to include in prompts:
- Your age
- Your investment experience (beginner, intermediate, advanced)
- Your risk tolerance (low, moderate, high)
- Your goals (retirement, wealth building, buying a house)
- Time frame (5 years, 20 years, etc.)
- How much you can invest

Sample Prompt

"I am 35 years old with a high-risk tolerance and want to invest $1,000/month for the next 25 years. What would a good, diversified ETF portfolio look like for long-term growth?"

This prompt is clear, providing your AI tool with specific information to work with.

One of the advantages of using AI is that you can ask follow-up questions. It remembers the conversation[2], so once you receive an answer, you can say the following:

- "Now compare those ETFs to international options."
- "What happens if I cut my monthly investment in half?"
- "Would adding a small-cap ETF improve diversification?"

Treat it like a conversation, not a one-off inquiry. Follow-up questions allow you to delve deeper, refine the output, and receive valuable information for informed decision making.

How to Structure Your Prompt

Prompts do not need to be elaborate, but a little structure can significantly aid AI in understanding your request and

---

2   AI tools like ChatGPT can remember parts of your conversation to keep things flowing naturally, especially during a single session. For example, if you ask a question about your portfolio and then follow up a few minutes later, AI can usually connect the dots. However, unless you are using a version of AI with long-term memory turned on, it will not remember past sessions once the chat ends. Even when memory is on, it is limited. It can remember what you have told it, but it does not know everything about your financial situation unless you share it. So, always double-check what it gives you and keep your sensitive information secure. You can find more about this in a later section.

delivering a better answer. A well-structured prompt clarifies what you want to know and how you would like the information presented: Would you prefer a comparison, a summary, a simulation, or a plain-English explanation? Think of it as providing AI with a blueprint rather than a blank canvas. You do not need to use technical terms or fancy formatting; just be clear and intentional. For example, prompts like "Compare VTI and SCHB on fees and performance" or "Summarize the pros and cons of investing in REITs" will yield more helpful responses than simply asking, "Tell me about these funds."[3] Moreover, a prompt like "Simulate a 70% stocks/30% bonds portfolio with $500 monthly contributions over 30 years at a 6% annual return" is also structured in a way that makes it easy for AI to give you something useful. Using formats like compare, summarize, simulate, and explain keeps your question focused, resulting in answers that are more targeted, digestible, and actionable.

You want to provide the AI tool with enough direction to be useful, but not so much that you restrict its ability to assist you. Think of it like telling your navigation system where you want to go—you do not need to mention every single turn, but you must be clear and realistic about where you are headed. If your prompt is too vague, AI will not understand what you are truly seeking. Conversely, if it is too detailed or rigid, you might miss out on the creative or valuable insights it could offer. The key is to give just enough context, such as your goal, risk tolerance, or time frame, while leaving room for AI to suggest opportunities and point out blind spots. The best prompts strike a balance between clarity and

---

3   VTI is the ticker symbol for the Vanguard Total Stock Market ETF, and SCHB is the ticker symbol for the Schwab US Broad Market ETF. Both are ETFs that provide diversified exposure to US equities. REITs stands for real estate investment trusts, which are companies that own, operate, or finance income-producing real estate.

flexibility, helping you explore your options without feeling over-whelmed or overly constrained. Consider the following examples:

Too Vague
- "How should I invest my money?"
- "Which stocks will go up?"
- "Tell me about retirement."

Unrealistic
- "Tell me what to buy now so that I can double my money in six months."
- "Which five stocks will beat the S&P 500 every year for the next decade?"
- "Give me the age I should retire and how much money I will need."

Just Right
- "Create three sample investment strategies for a 40-year-old with a high risk tolerance who can invest $1,000 per month for the next 20 years."
- "Summarize the historical performance, fees, and risks of VTI and SCHB to help me compare them as potential core holdings."
- "Outline the key steps someone in their early 50s should take if they want to retire at age 65, including savings goals, portfolio allocation, and Social Security considerations."

Clear Beats Complex

When communicating with AI, avoid trying to impress it with technical jargon or academic phrasing; plain language works best. What matters most is that your prompt is clear and easy to understand. Consider how you would explain your question to a smart friend who is not in finance. You want to be direct, specific, and goal-oriented. Instead of saying, "Analyze the volatility-adjusted return profile of my multi-asset allocation," you could simply ask, "Is my portfolio too risky based on how much it has fluctuated lately?" You will often get a better, more actionable answer with that second phrasing. The goal is to obtain helpful information, not to sound sophisticated.

Using simple terms makes prompting faster, more natural, and more likely to give you something you can actually use. AI is designed to understand everyday language. You can say things like "I am 30 years old, want to retire at age 60, and can save $1,000 a month—what kind of plan should I follow?" and you will get something solid in return. You do not need to over-think it or mimic the language of Wall Street. The more honest and specific your questions are, the more real and relevant the answers will be. That's the power of simple wording—it gets straight to the point and makes AI feel less like a robot and more like a smart assistant sitting across the table from you.

Good Prompt in Simple Terms
- "I am 28 years old, new to investing, and want to build a basic portfolio using index funds. What do you recommend I start with?"

Using a straightforward prompt like this will yield a solid answer without needing to reference technical terms.

Sample Prompts to Try

Now that you know how to write effective prompts, you are in control. Do not hesitate to tweak or refine them, as there is no single perfect version. Edit as you go, adjust based on the responses you get back, and enjoy the process. The more you experiment, the better you will become at unlocking useful, creative, and even surprising results. Below are additional examples of investing prompts categorized by topic:

Retirement Planning

- "Create a retirement savings plan for someone who is 30 years old, wants to retire at age 60 with $1 million, and can invest $750 per month. Assume a 7% annual return and account for inflation."
- "How much would a 35-year-old need to invest each month to reach $3 million by age 67, assuming an average annual return of 8% and no existing savings?"

Fund Selection

- "Compare FZROX, VTSAX, and SWTSX in terms of expense ratios, diversification across sectors and market caps, tax efficiency in taxable accounts, and minimum investment requirements."[4]
- "Recommend three bond ETFs with low expense ratios, solid credit quality, and consistent historical returns over the past 10 years. Include fund duration and yield."[5]

---

4   FZROX (Fidelity ZERO Total Market Index Fund), VTSAX (Vanguard Total Stock Market Index Fund Admiral Shares), and SWTSX (Schwab Total Stock Market Index Fund) are all mutual fund versions of total market index funds that cover US stocks across sectors and company sizes. Since these are mutual funds, comparable ETFs may be more tax-efficient in taxable accounts.

5   Duration tells you how sensitive a bond or bond fund is to changes in interest rates. A higher duration means the price moves more when rates change. Yield is the income you earn from holding that bond or fund, expressed as a percentage. A higher yield usually means more income, but it can also come with more risk.

Asset Allocation[6]

- "What is a suitable ETF allocation for a conservative investor with a 10-year investment horizon who prioritizes capital preservation but still wants some growth?"
- "Build a globally diversified portfolio using low-cost ETFs. Include specific fund recommendations for US stocks, international developed markets, and emerging markets."

Simulation and Scenario Planning

- "Simulate a $1,000 per month investment into a 70% stock/30% bond portfolio over 20 years. Show projected ending balance, range of outcomes, and impact of different return scenarios."
- "Model how an 80% stocks/20% bonds portfolio would have performed during the 2008 financial crisis versus a 60% stocks/40% bonds portfolio. Include peak-to-trough drawdowns[7] and recovery periods."

Risk Assessment

- "What are the key risks associated with investing in high-yield bond ETFs, including credit risk, interest rate sensitivity, and liquidity?"

---

6 Asset allocation refers to figuring out how to split your money across things like stocks, bonds, and cash so you are not putting all your eggs in one basket. The goal is to manage risk and aim for a return that fits your goals and comfort level. I will delve deeper into this later.

7 Peak-to-trough refers to the decline between the highest point (peak) and the lowest point (trough) of a market cycle or asset price. It helps show how much value was lost during a downturn before recovery began. Investors often use it to measure drawdowns or understand the depth of past corrections. Larger or more frequent drawdowns can indicate higher risk or volatility.

- "Explain the trade-offs between taking on more risk for higher long-term returns. Include how it affects volatility, drawdowns, and emotional decision-making during downturns."

Tax Efficiency

- "Which types of investments (e.g., index funds, bonds, REITs) are best held in a Roth IRA, traditional IRA, and taxable brokerage account based on tax efficiency, growth potential, and income treatment?"[8]
- "Create a sample asset location plan for someone with $100,000 in a Roth IRA, $250,000 in a traditional IRA, and $150,000 in a taxable brokerage account. Prioritize tax efficiency and long-term growth."
- "I am 35 years old. Based on a W-2 salary of $180,000 and $70,000 in net self-employment income, calculate the maximum allowed contributions to all tax-advantaged accounts for the current tax year. Include breakdowns for Solo 401(k) employee and employer contributions, HSA limits, and Roth IRA (or backdoor Roth) eligibility."[9]

---

8 An IRA (individual retirement account) is a retirement account with tax perks. A traditional IRA lets you put in pre-tax money, but withdrawals (including required minimum distributions or RMDs) are taxed later. A Roth IRA is the opposite – you contribute after-tax money, but qualified withdrawals are tax-free and there are no RMDs. Contribution limits apply each year and Roth eligibility depends on your income.

9 A 401(k) is an employer-sponsored retirement account that lets you save and invest with tax advantages where contributions can be pre-tax (traditional) or after-tax (Roth) and many employers offer a match. A Solo 401(k) works the same way, but is designed for self-employed individuals, allowing both "employee" and "employer" contributions to boost savings. An HSA (health savings account) is another tax-advantaged option, available if you have a high-deductible health plan, and it offers triple tax benefits: deductible contributions, tax-free growth, and tax-free withdrawals for qualified medical expenses.

Use AI to Learn, Not Just Decide

An overlooked way to use tools like ChatGPT is as a tutor, not just a shortcut to an answer. If you are curious about something, such as how dividends work, why people diversify globally, or what risk-adjusted returns mean, ask it to break the concept down. Once you understand the basics, follow up. Ask for examples, inquire about pros and cons, or explore how it applies to your situation. You are not just collecting facts; you are building intuition. Investing is one of those fields where your confidence grows with understanding and experience, and AI is excellent at walking you through the learning curve as you gain experience over time.

Let's say you are wondering whether to reinvest dividends or take the cash. You could ask AI to explain the concept, then take it further: "What is the impact of dividend reinvestment over 20 years?" or "Are there situations where it's better not to reinvest?" That kind of layered learning gives you not just a surface-level takeaway but a deeper grasp of how different decisions play out. It is like having a patient teacher who doesn't get annoyed when you ask your tenth follow-up question. You can simply keep digging until it clicks.

This kind of back-and-forth builds not just knowledge but financial confidence. It transforms AI from a mere recommendation engine into a tool that helps you understand the why behind the what. Once you know why something matters, you are less likely to be thrown off course when markets get bumpy or headlines get messy. You will feel grounded in your decisions because you understand them, not just because someone—or something—told you what to do. That's the kind of lesson that stays with you.

Personalize It

Another powerful way to use AI for investing guidance is by combining your prompts with real data, particularly your own. Instead of keeping things hypothetical, bring your actual numbers to the table. Upload your current portfolio, list the funds in your 401(k), or outline your monthly budget. The more context you provide, the more personalized and helpful the feedback becomes. Think of it like meeting with a financial advisor: the more they know about your financial picture, the better advice they can give. AI works similarly. It doesn't need to guess your situation if you provide the necessary information upfront.

Let's say you are looking at your 401(k) options and feeling overwhelmed. You could say, "Here are my plan's fund options. Help me build a diversified portfolio for moderate risk." Alternatively, perhaps you are unsure if you are saving enough, in which case, you could say, "Based on my income of $85,000, fixed expenses of $3,200/month, and variable expenses of $1,000/month, how much should I be saving toward retirement if I want to stop working at age 60?" These types of prompts give AI a framework to work with, resulting in a tailored recommendation rather than just generic advice.

You can also ask AI to audit what you are already doing. Try: "Review this portfolio for diversification and tax efficiency" or "Tell me if these fund choices align with a long-term growth strategy." If you have cash sitting on the sidelines, you could upload a snapshot of your accounts and ask, "Based on my current asset allocation, where should I deploy this extra $25,000?"[10] This turns AI into a second set of eyes—one that

---

10   More on this later, but when sharing information with AI, avoid uploading full account statements or anything with personal identifiers.

can help you spot gaps, opportunities, or areas that could be optimized. It won't replace due diligence, but it can act like a coach, helping you think through your options more clearly.

Besides, it is not just about investments. You can use AI to assist with debt repayment, budgeting, or even deciding between buying a home and renting. For example, "Here is my credit card balance, student loans, and monthly income—what is the best strategy to pay this off?" or "Given my down payment savings, current rent, and housing market conditions, should I consider buying or keep renting for another year?" These are the real-life, day-to-day financial decisions most of us face, and AI can walk you through the trade-offs, numbers, and outcomes step by step. The more personal you make the prompt, the more practical the answer becomes.

Common Mistakes to Avoid

Being Too Vague
- Instead of asking "Tell me about investing," try something more focused: "What are the basics of starting an investment portfolio using index funds for long-term growth?"

Not Giving Context
- AI doesn't know your age, income, or risk tolerance unless you tell it.

Overloading the Prompt
- Break big questions into smaller pieces. Ask about one thing at a time.

Expecting a Crystal Ball

- AI can simulate and forecast, but it cannot predict the future.

Failing to Follow Up

- Use follow-ups to refine, compare, and expand.

Prompting is a skill; the more you practice, the better you become. After a while, you will find a rhythm and receive more helpful responses faster. Don't hesitate to edit your questions, ask again, or try a new angle. That's how you turn AI into a powerful investing assistant. Remember, AI is a tool that does not replace your judgment or your responsibility, but it can help you make more informed decisions. The goal isn't to blindly follow AI's advice but to use it to explore your options, test your ideas, and grow your financial confidence. If you can ask good questions, you can get good answers. That can make all the difference in investing.

CHAPTER 3

PRINCIPLES OF INVESTING YOU SHOULD NOT (AND CANNOT) AUTOMATE

"Machines are excellent at analysis.
Humans must still supply the wisdom."
—*Adapted from Ray Dalio's Principles*

AI can scan thousands of data points in seconds, crunch numbers faster than any spreadsheet you have ever built, and summarize an entire portfolio's historical risk in moments. However, even with all that horsepower, there are some aspects of investing that AI should never replace. This is because successful long-term investing is not just about numbers but also about goals, preferences, values, discipline, and emotions. That is the human side of money, which cannot be outsourced to a machine.

AI is a tool, and a powerful one at that. It can help you compare funds, suggest allocations, test scenarios, or identify risks you might not see on your own. However, it cannot make decisions for you. Those still require thought, reflection, and context. In this chapter, we will walk through the investing principles that you—the investor—need to own. These are the parts that should never be fully automated, no matter how advanced technology gets.

Goals Cannot Be Automated

A good investment strategy starts with a purpose. That purpose is personal. It might be saving for retirement, buying a house, funding your child's education, or simply building financial security. Whatever it is, your plan needs to be built around your purpose. AI can't tell you what matters most to you. It does not know how you feel about having financial independence at the age of 50 as opposed to helping your aging parents or launching a business in five years. It can't prioritize your values.

Strong financial plans are goal-based because money should be working toward something. Investing isn't just math; it's also matching your dollars to your life. Once you've identified your goal(s), AI can help reverse-engineer the plan. It can tell you how much to save, what rate of return you want to aim for, and which portfolio structures can support your timeline. However, you have to supply the goal(s), otherwise, you're just optimizing in a vacuum.

Risk Tolerance: Know Yourself Before You Ask AI

Risk tolerance is not something you can plug into a calculator and forget. It's one of the most personal and misunderstood parts of investing. Yes, AI can estimate your risk profile (see

Chapter 6). It can also group you into a model portfolio labeled "conservative," "moderate," or "aggressive." However, that does not mean much unless you have taken the time to understand how you respond to risk.

Two people can be the same age, with the same income, have the same asset mix, and still react completely differently when the stock market drops by 20%. One might see it as a buying opportunity, while the other might want to sell everything. That reaction is emotional, not mathematical. This is why risk tolerance depends more on psychology and behavior than purely on a score on a risk tolerance questionnaire. A computer does not panic regardless of whether the NASDAQ[11] is up or down, nor does it lose sleep over market corrections. That is why it is important to be completely honest with yourself when framing and defining your risk tolerance. Once you understand how much risk you can handle and how much you need to take to reach your goals, you can use AI to model scenarios and help you find the right balance. You should guide that process, not let the technology decide for you. You'll find more on this later.

Time Horizon: Context Is Everything

Investing without a clear time horizon is like training for a race without knowing if it's a sprint or a marathon. Your timeline affects everything—from the assets you choose to how you respond to market swings. AI tools can do a great job simulating

---

11 The NASDAQ is a major US stock exchange known for its focus on technology and growth companies. It lists firms like Apple, Microsoft, and Amazon and is often used as a benchmark for the performance of the information technology sector.

outcomes over different time frames, but they cannot decide how long you plan to keep your money invested.

If you are saving to buy a house in three years, AI might suggest a conservative mix that protects your principal. Alternatively, if you are investing for retirement 30 years from now, it may recommend a growth-heavy portfolio. Both recommendations might be correct based on the data, but only you know when you might need the money and how much flexibility you have.

Time horizon is also what gives compound interest its power. The earlier you start, the less you have to contribute to reach the same goal. That's not something AI needs to tell you, but it can help you visualize the difference that time makes. What it cannot do is decide if early retirement is worth the trade-offs or if you are willing to wait longer for a higher payoff. Those are personal decisions.

Diversification and Asset Allocation: Use AI to Analyze, Not Decide

You can begin thinking about portfolio construction after your goals, risk tolerance, and time horizon are clear. This is where diversification and asset allocation are crucial. AI can absolutely help here by running countless simulations, calculating correlation matrices, and suggesting optimized allocations based on your profile. But again, the final decision is still yours.

Diversification is about avoiding putting all your eggs in one basket. You already knew that, but here's where the nuance lies: just because you own a dozen ETFs does not mean you are as diversified as you may think. AI might suggest five funds, but if they all own a lot of the same tech giants (i.e., Apple,

Microsoft, Nvidia, Amazon, Meta, Alphabet, and Tesla), then your portfolio may be more concentrated than you think, even if it does not look that way on paper. This is where you need to step in and examine what's really driving your investments.

Asset allocation—or how much you put in stocks, bonds, real estate, cash, and other categories—is arguably one of the most important decisions you'll make regarding investing. It has more impact on long-term returns than picking the perfect stock. AI can help illustrate the trade-offs: more stocks can mean more growth potential but also more volatility, whereas more bonds can mean more stability but lower expected returns. Only you can weigh those trade-offs.

AI Cannot Predict the Future, and Neither Can You

One of the most tempting misuses of AI in investing is treating it like a crystal ball, which it is not. Yes, it can simulate market returns based on historical patterns, and it can also forecast how your portfolio might behave under different economic scenarios, but those are models, not guarantees. They are based on the past, not the future.

Don't get me wrong—this kind of modeling is useful. It can help you stress-test your portfolio as you prepare for different possible outcomes. However, it should never be mistaken for certainty. AI can help you think through what might happen, but it cannot tell you what will happen. Any tool that claims otherwise should be treated with caution. A significant part of investing is living with uncertainty. That's why long-term planning, diversification, and emotional control matter. AI can support all of those things, but it does not remove the uncertainty itself. No one can.

Emotions Matter, and AI Doesn't Have Any

This is one of the biggest reasons to keep the human element front and center. Investing is an emotional endeavor. We all like to think we are rational, logical decision-makers, but the truth contradicts that. We get excited when markets go up and nervous when they go down. We also chase trends, panic during crashes, and overreact to headlines. That's just human nature.

AI does not feel any of that, which can be helpful. It can provide you with a calm, data-driven perspective when you are stressed. Moreover, it can remind you of your long-term plan and re-run your projections to show you that you are still on track, even after a bad quarter. However, it cannot talk you out of selling at the bottom, nor can it convince you to stick to your plan when everyone else is panicking. That part is on you. That's why discipline is one of the few things in investing you truly cannot outsource. AI can be a sounding board, a second opinion, or even a coach, but it's not you, and you still are the decision-maker.

Stay in the Driver's Seat

AI is a powerful navigator, but you're still the one driving the car. The core principles of investing—clarifying your goals, knowing your risk tolerance, understanding your time horizon, building a diversified portfolio, and staying disciplined—are human decisions. They always have been, and they should stay that way. Machines can analyze, but humans must decide. This is not necessarily a weakness. When you combine the best of both worlds—that is, your wisdom and AI's capabilities—you can build a smarter investing strategy. Just don't hand over the keys.

CHAPTER 4

WHAT ARE YOUR GOALS?

"A goal without a plan is just a wish."
—*Antoine de Saint-Exupéry*

Financial success does not start with spreadsheets but with knowing what you want. You cannot make progress if you do not know where you are trying to go. That is why setting goals is the foundation of everything we do in financial planning. Whether your objective is to build wealth, become debt-free, travel more, buy a home, or retire early, your money needs direction. Without it, you may be chasing random outcomes instead of building the life you want.

Your Goals Give Your Money Purpose

When people think about financial planning, they often jump straight to the numbers: budgets, investments, and savings rates. Those certainly are important, but they are merely tools.

Your goals are the purpose behind the tools. They are the reason you are putting money away, investing for the future, or paying off debt. Whether you're aiming for financial independence, saving for a down payment, or building a college fund, clear goals help you prioritize, focus, and measure progress.

Here's where AI comes in. Using tools like ChatGPT, you can turn vague hopes into structured, step-by-step plans. The right prompt can help you outline a timeline, quantify your target, and explore different strategies based on your income, lifestyle, and preferences. So, think of AI not as a replacement for planning but as your brainstorming partner. It's here to guide you, help with the math, and assist you in thinking through the trade-offs.

Unclear Hopes Will Not Cut It

We all want more financial security, but vague aspirations like "I want to be rich" or "I don't want to worry about money" are not actionable. Such statements don't tell you how much to save, what to invest in, or what to prioritize. Conversely, clear, defined goals give your money a job, helping you avoid lifestyle inflation, make smarter spending choices, and stay committed when things get tough.

It is also easier to stick to your plan when you know what you're working toward. Sacrificing happy hours or skipping a vacation doesn't feel like deprivation if it means getting closer to a goal that truly matters, like owning your first home or being debt-free. When you frame your goals in time-based, measurable terms, you create accountability. That is why goal setting isn't just "nice to have"—it is essential.

Break Your Goals Down by Timeline

To make goal planning easier, divide your goals into three categories:

- Short-Term Goals (Under one year): These are short-term priorities, such as building an emergency fund or paying off a lower credit card balance.
- Medium-Term Goals (1–5 years): These might include saving for a home, buying a car with cash, paying down student loans, or launching a business.
- Long-Term Goals (5+ years): These are where you plan for college savings, retirement, or financial independence.

Once you categorize your goals by timeline, you can better match them with the right strategy and the right tools (like a high-yield savings account for short-term needs or ETFs for long-term growth). A powerful way to bring clarity to your goals is to make them SMART[12]:

- Specific: What exactly do you want?
- Measurable: How much money will it take?
- Achievable: Is the goal realistic based on your income and time frame?
- Relevant: Does it align with your overall priorities?
- Time-Bound: What's the deadline?

For example, "I want to save for a home" becomes "I want to save $25,000 in four years for a down payment on a $250,000 house." This is where AI excels and can help you sharpen your goals, run the numbers, and offer suggestions you might not

---

12   Doran, G. T. (1981). There's a S.M.A.R.T. way to write management's goals and objectives. *Management Review*, 70(11), 35–36.

have considered. Below are sample prompts organized by goal type and time frame.

Short-Term SMART Goal Prompts (Under One Year)

Usually, these goals focus on building a financial safety net or preparing for upcoming expenses. They're mostly savings-based, not investment-based.

- "Help me create a six-month savings plan to build a $1,500 emergency fund on a $4,000/month income."
- "How can I pay off $2,000 in credit card debt in four months while still covering my bills?"
- "Create a monthly budget to save $500 for holiday travel by December."
- "What's the best way to set aside $200/month for car maintenance over the next nine months?"
- "Build a plan to cover a job transition without taking on more debt."

With these prompts, AI can build a step-by-step savings plan, forecast trade-offs, and adjust timelines if needed. It can even simulate different payoff strategies, like snowball versus avalanche for debt, as we will see in an upcoming chapter.[13]

---

13 The debt snowball method means paying off your smallest debts first to build momentum and motivation while making minimum payments on the rest. The avalanche method focuses instead on paying off the highest interest debts first to minimize total interest paid over time. Both approaches can work, so choose the one that keeps you consistent and moving forward.

Medium-Term SMART Goal Prompts (1–5 Years)

These goals often involve balancing saving, debt reduction, and potentially investing. They require a little more planning and prioritization.

- "How can I save $25,000 in four years for a down payment on a house?"
- "Give me a three-year plan to pay off $30,000 in student loans with a $60,000 salary."
- "Create a strategy to buy a $20,000 car with cash in two years."
- "Help me invest to grow $10,000 into $15,000 in three years with moderate risk."
- "I want to launch a small business in four years with $50,000. How should I start saving?"

Here, AI can help balance competing goals, recommend asset allocations based on time horizon and risk, and suggest budgeting strategies to stay on track.

Long-Term SMART Goal Prompts (5+ Years)

These are the big-picture financial goals, such as retirement or financial independence. The focus here shifts from saving to investing and optimizing for growth.

- "How much should I invest monthly to retire with $1 million in 30 years?"
- "Create a plan to save $100,000 in 10 years for my child's college expenses."
- "What's a realistic plan to pay off my mortgage in 15 years instead of 30 years?"

- "If I want to start my own business in six years, how much should I save annually?"
- "Help me plan to reach financial independence by age 55."

These goals are ideal for combining with AI's forecasting and backtesting capabilities. You can simulate different return assumptions, savings rates, and timelines to build a plan that fits your life. More on this to come.

Balancing Competing Goals

Life is rarely as neat as a single goal on a timeline. Most of us are juggling a handful of financial priorities all at once. Perhaps you are trying to pay off debt, invest for retirement, and still take the occasional vacation to the beach with your family. That is a lot to manage. This is where AI really shines: it can help you step back, weigh the trade-offs, and build a realistic, personalized roadmap that accounts for your income, expenses, and time horizons. You can ask it things like "How do I balance saving for a house with investing for retirement?" or "What should I tackle first, credit card debt or student loans?" AI won't make the decision for you, but it will lay out the options in simple terms so that you can make informed choices based on your own priorities.

Competing Goals Sample Prompts

- "Can you help me balance saving for a house, investing for retirement, and starting a business?"

- "Should I prioritize saving for retirement or paying off credit card debt?"
- "What are the opportunity costs of paying off my mortgage early versus investing the extra money?"
- "What am I missing in my financial goals based on my age, income, and timeline?"

Example Prompt with Output and Interpretation

Prompt

"Should I prioritize saving for retirement or paying off credit card debt?"

AI Response

In most cases, paying off high-interest credit card debt should come first, especially if interest rates are 15–25%. That debt compounds quickly and can sabotage your progress. A smart prioritization strategy often looks like the following:

- Make minimum payments on all debts.
- Build a $500–$1,000 emergency fund.
- Pay off high-interest debt.
- Contribute enough to your 401(k) to get an employer match.
- Once credit card debt is gone, ramp up retirement savings.

Interpretation

When you are deciding between paying off debt or saving for retirement, the math is clear: start with the credit cards. With high credit card interest rates, that balance is growing faster than nearly any investment you could make. Cover the minimums on all debts, set aside a small emergency fund, and attack those credit cards with focus. Once the high-interest balances are out of the way, shift gears and put money into your 401(k)—at least enough to capture any employer match. From there, you can increase retirement contributions.

Big Decisions Made Clearer with the Help of AI

One of the most effective ways to use AI for financial goal planning is to let it walk you through trade-offs and explore a range of what-if scenarios.[14] So much of personal finance isn't black and white but rather gray and full of tough choices. AI gives you the ability to test those choices in a low-stakes environment and see how they play out over time. For instance, you can ask, "What happens if I delay retirement by five years?" or "How much does it really matter if I start investing at 25 years old versus 35 years old?" Instead of guessing, you receive clear projections and explanations that help you understand the long-term impact of each decision.

For example, let's say you are investing $300 a month and wondering whether it is enough. Ask AI to model your

---

14   Chapter 10 discusses this in greater detail.

progress toward a retirement target with that contribution and then show how things change if you bumped it up to $500 or started five years earlier. You are not just crunching numbers; you are testing different paths and seeing which one aligns best with your life. You can also factor in real-world considerations, like market returns, inflation, or unexpected expenses, to make your planning more realistic.

Another great use is comparing big decisions like renting and buying a home. You can enter your city, rent amount, potential home cost, interest rates, property taxes, and even estimate maintenance costs. Then, ask AI to compare the financial impact over the next 10 or 15 years. It will walk you through the total cost, opportunity cost (like what your down payment could earn if invested), and any tax advantages. That kind of side-by-side comparison is incredibly valuable when you are facing a significant financial fork in the road.

These kinds of prompts are not just for number crunching but for building confidence. When you understand how your choices affect your future, you're less likely to second-guess yourself. Whether you are trying to save for retirement, plan for a big purchase, or simply make better use of your income, AI can help you stress-test different paths so you can make smarter, more informed decisions.

At the end of the day, goal setting might seem basic, but it is critical in financial planning. Goals provide your money with direction, helping you stay focused, motivated, and grounded when life throws curveballs. Without clear goals, it is easy to drift by saving a little here and spending a little there, never knowing if you are getting closer to the life you want. A financial plan without goals is like a navigation system with no destination. You might move, but you will not know if you are heading in the right direction.

CHAPTER 5

CURRENT FINANCIAL SITUATION

"Do not save what is left after spending,
but spend what is left after saving."
—*Warren Buffett*

Before building any kind of financial plan, selecting an investment, or thinking about retirement, you need to know where you stand right now. This means taking a clear, honest look at your current financial situation—not what you hope it is or wish it could be, but what it actually is. This chapter is all about clarity. It focuses on getting your financial snapshot in order so you can stop guessing and start making decisions based on facts. The good news? You don't have to do it alone. Today, AI tools can do a lot of the heavy lifting when it comes to organizing your finances. But even with the help of technology, the first move is yours.

Track Where Your Money Goes

The simplest place to begin is your income. How much do you bring in each month after taxes? If your income fluctuates, take an average of the last 6–12 months. Don't inflate the numbers—be honest. You are not trying to impress anyone here; you're trying to get a handle on the truth. Make sure to include bonuses, investment income, or rental income if it is consistent. The point is to understand what resources you have to work with.

The next is the question: Where is your money going? This is where people are often surprised. You might think you are spending $400 on food when it is closer to $1,000 once you add up takeout, coffee, and DoorDash. That's fine. This is not about feeling guilt but gaining awareness.

Start by breaking expenses into the following categories:
- Fixed expenses (rent/mortgage payment, insurance, car note)
- Variable essentials (gas, groceries, utilities)
- Discretionary (restaurants, travel, shopping)
- Savings and investments

Once you understand where your money is going, the next step is to review your liabilities, including the following:
- Credit cards
- Student loans
- Car loans
- Mortgages
- Personal loans

Record the current balance, minimum monthly payment, and interest rate for each. This lets you calculate your total monthly obligations and your weighted average interest rate.

Looking at your liabilities isn't fun, but now we turn our attention to your assets. An asset is anything you own that has value and can be converted into cash. This includes things like cash, real estate, stocks, retirement accounts, and even personal property with resale value. In financial planning, assets are used to measure your net worth and determine your ability to reach future financial goals. Add up the assets that you own, which may include:

- checking and savings accounts,
- retirement and brokerage accounts,
- home or other real estate (use conservative estimates),
- vehicles (resale value), and
- other valuables or business equity.

This tells you what you have working for you or what you could potentially access in an emergency. Now that you know what you owe and what you own, subtract your total liabilities from your total assets. The resulting number is your net worth and comprises your personal balance sheet.[15] Do not worry if it's negative—what matters is that you know it and can track it moving forward. Tracking your net worth over time is one of the best ways to measure your progress and is what typically distinguishes someone as a "millionaire."[16] It won't move

---

15 A balance sheet is a snapshot of what you own and what you owe at a specific point in time. For businesses, it shows assets (like cash, inventory, and equipment), liabilities (like loans and unpaid bills), and the owner's equity. For individuals, it lists your assets (like savings, investments, and property), debts (like credit cards and mortgages), and net worth, which is the difference between the two.

16 A millionaire is someone whose net worth, meaning their total assets minus any debts, equals one million dollars or more. It does not necessarily mean they have a million dollars in cash; it simply means that if they

every day, but it should trend upward over time if your plan is working.

Next, focus on your personal income statement.[17] Take your total income and subtract your total expenses. The difference is your cash flow. If you are in the black each month (i.e., have money leftover), great. Now calculate your savings rate: how much are you saving or investing each month as a percentage of your income? The higher the savings rate, the faster you can build wealth. A good target is 15–25%, but any positive savings rate is better than nothing.

At this point, you can pull all this together into a personal financial statement. This is a snapshot of the following, usually conveyed in one page:

- Total income
- Total expenses
- Monthly surplus or deficit
- Savings rate
- List of assets
- List of liabilities
- Net worth

AI can help with all of the previous steps and categorization of items by cleaning up your data, summarizing your financial picture, and helping you create systems that work. You still have to do the thinking, but instead of spending hours formatting

---

sold everything they own and paid off all of their liabilities, they would have at least a million dollars left over.

17   A personal income statement shows how much you earn, how much you spend, and what is left over at the end. It follows the same idea as a company's income statement, where revenues minus expenses equals profit, but it applies to your own finances. Rather than tracking sales or costs of goods, you track your income and spending to see whether you are living within your means or not.

spreadsheets, you can focus on making better decisions with the proper financial information.

Income and Cash Flow Sample Prompts

* "I earn $85,000 per year and live in [State]. Estimate my take-home pay after federal, state, and local taxes. Assume I take the standard deduction and have no dependents. Show monthly and annual after-tax income."
* "I expect to receive a $[X] bonus this quarter. Suggest ways to allocate it between short-term goals (like debt or spending), long-term goals (like investing or saving), and taxes."
* "Based on my monthly income of $[X] and recurring expenses of $[Y] (including housing, bills, debt payments, and spending), calculate my free cash flow each month. Highlight areas where I could improve cash flow if needed."

Example Prompt with Output and Interpretation

Prompt

Enter your per-month income after taxes and recurring expenses.

"Based on my income and recurring expenses, calculate how much free cash flow I have left at the end of each month."

AI Response

Let's say your monthly after-tax income is $5,000. Your recurring monthly expenses break down as follows:

- Rent: $1,500
- Utilities and internet: $250
- Groceries: $600
- Transportation (car payment, gas, insurance): $550
- Subscriptions and memberships: $150
- Minimum debt payments: $400
- Health insurance: $250
- Miscellaneous spending: $300

Your total recurring expenses equal $4,000/month, which leaves you with $1,000 in free cash flow. This is money you can allocate toward savings, investing, extra debt payments, or discretionary spending.

Interpretation

This prompt helps you figure out how much money is left over after all your regular bills are paid each month. We start with your after-tax income—that is, what actually hits your bank account—and subtract the necessary expenses like rent, food, and transportation. That leftover amount is free cash flow and is a measure of how much flexibility you have in your budget.

In the example above, with $5,000 in income and $4,000 in recurring expenses, you end up with $1,000 of free cash each month. This leftover money can be put toward growing your savings, investing, paying down debt faster, or even spending on things you enjoy. Knowing your free cash flow helps you avoid overspending and gives you clarity on how quickly you can reach your financial goals.

Spending and Budgeting Sample Prompts

- "Using the 50/30/20 rule, build a budget for me based on a monthly after-tax income of $4,500."
"I am planning for a major expense (e.g., a wedding or vacation) in six months; how should I adjust my monthly budget to prepare?"
- "Categorize my last 50 credit card transactions into spending groups (e.g., groceries, housing, dining, subscriptions, transportation, entertainment, and other)."
- "What percentage of my income am I spending on needs versus wants versus savings?"
- "Create a monthly budget for me based on my current income and average expenses."
- "Help me adjust my budget to save an additional $200/month without cutting essentials."

Example Prompt with Output and Interpretation

Prompt
"Using the 50/30/20 rule, build a budget for me based on a monthly after-tax income of $4,500."

AI Response
The 50/30/20 rule divides your after-tax income into three main categories:
- 50% Needs: $2,250—rent, utilities, groceries, transportation, insurance, minimum loan payments
- 30% Wants: $1,350—dining out, entertainment, travel, shopping, subscriptions

---

- 20% Savings/Debt Repayment: $900—emergency fund, investing, extra loan payments
- So, for a monthly income of $4,500, you'd aim to spend:
  - o no more than $2,250 on essentials;
  - o up to $1,350 on discretionary spending; and
  - o at least $900 toward saving or paying off debt faster.

Interpretation

This output demonstrates how to apply a popular budgeting framework, the 50/30/20 rule, to organize your finances. The idea is to divide your income into three manageable categories: needs (essentials), wants (discretionary), and savings (which includes investing). If you earn $4,500 each month after taxes, you should aim to limit essential expenses, such as rent and groceries, to about $2,250. Spending on wants should be capped at $1,350; however, if you can spend less in this area each month, you can free up more money for debt reduction and/or saving and investing. This strategy can help you get out of debt faster and/or build your investments sooner.

Debt Assessment Sample Prompts

- List all of your current debts, including the following details: outstanding balance, interest rate, minimum monthly payment, and due date for each. "Based on this information, recommend which debts I should prioritize paying off first to reduce interest costs and financial stress."

- "Explain the snowball and avalanche methods for paying off credit card debt and which is preferred, given I have two credit cards and one has a balance of $[X] and an interest rate of [X%] and the other a balance of $[Y] and an interest rate of [Y%]."
- "If I increase my monthly credit card payment from $150 to $300, calculate how much faster I will pay off the balance and how much interest I will save over time. Use an interest rate of [X%] and an initial balance of $[X]. Show the difference in payoff time and total interest paid."
- "Based on my monthly income of $[X] and recurring expenses of $[Y], calculate how much I can realistically allocate toward debt payments each month without jeopardizing my emergency savings, investment contributions, or other financial goals. Suggest a sustainable payment plan."
- "I have a mix of student loans, car loans, and credit card balances. Based on my income, expenses, and current debt details (balances, interest rates, minimums), build a clear, step-by-step payoff plan that includes monthly payment targets, payoff order, and tips to expedite the process. Help me stay on track while still covering essentials."

Example Prompt with Output and Interpretation

Prompt

"Explain the snowball and avalanche methods for paying off credit card debt and which is preferred, given I have two credit cards and one has a balance of $3,200 and an interest rate of 29.99% and the other a balance of $1,400 and an interest rate of 25.99%."

AI Response

Debt Snowball Method
- List debts from smallest balance to largest balance.
- Pay the minimum on both cards.
- Apply all extra money to the card with the smallest balance first.
- Once the $1,400 card is gone, roll its payment into the $3,200 card.
- Pros: You get a quick win by eliminating the $1,400 card fast, which can be very motivating.
- Cons: You'll pay more in total interest, since you aren't tackling the highest-rate card first.

Debt Avalanche Method
- List debts from the highest interest rate to the lowest interest rate.
- Pay the minimum on both cards.
- Apply all additional money to the 29.99% card (the $3,200 balance).
- Once it's gone, roll that payment into the $1,400 card at 25.99%.
- Pros: This saves you the most money, because you're targeting the debt with the higher rate first.
- Cons: You'll have to wait longer before you completely eliminate one balance, which may feel less rewarding in the short term.

Which Is Preferred Here?
- Snowball: Faster psychological win (you clear the $1,400 card quickly)
- Avalanche: Financially smarter (you reduce interest costs by paying down the 29.99% card first)

Bottom line: If your top priority is saving money on interest, choose Avalanche. If your priority is motivation and quick progress, choose Snowball.

Interpretation

Managing debt can be stressful and draining and, at times, feel like you're just treading water no matter how much you pay. When you're deciding between the snowball and avalanche methods, the difference really comes down to what keeps you motivated versus what saves you the most money. Both strategies work, but in this case, the avalanche method saves you more in the long run, while the snowball method gives you a quick win. It is less about the math in situations like this and more about knowing which payoff style you will actually stick with.

Net Worth and Personal Financial Statement Sample Prompts

- "Here is a breakdown of my current asset mix across cash, stocks, bonds, retirement accounts, real estate, and other holdings. Based on my age [insert age] and risk tolerance [low/medium/high], how does this compare to a recommended allocation? Suggest adjustments if I am underweight or overweight in certain areas."
- "Build a personal financial statement summary with three sections: assets, liabilities, and net worth, using the data I provide."
- "If I increase my monthly savings by $500 and earn an average return of 6% annually, how will this affect my

net worth over the next five years? Assume the savings are invested monthly and returns are compounded. Provide both a table and a visual chart if possible."

- "Based on my age [insert age] and income [insert income], how does my current net worth compare to national averages or percentiles? Use reliable sources like the Federal Reserve or Census data, and include where I fall relative to national averages. Help me understand what that means in context."

- "Here is a list of my debts and other liabilities. Identify which ones are having the most significant negative impact on my net worth based on interest rates, balances, or cash flow burden. Then, suggest strategies to reduce or restructure these liabilities to improve my financial health."

Example Prompt with Output and Interpretation

Scenario: Jake and Maya

- Age: 38 and 36
- Children: 2
- Occupations: Jake is an engineer ($130K/year); Maya is a part-time nurse ($50K/year)

Prompt

"Build a personal financial statement summary with three sections: assets, liabilities, and net worth, using the data I provide."

The data provided is as follows:

Assets
- Checking Account: $6,000
- Emergency Fund (High-Yield Savings): $24,000
- 401(k) – Jake: $112,000
- Roth IRA – Maya: $38,000
- Brokerage Account: $27,000
- Home Market Value: $415,000
- Two Vehicles (Combined Resale Value): $22,000

Liabilities
- Mortgage Balance: $298,000
- Student Loans (Maya): $14,000
- Car Loan (Jake's SUV): $9,500
- Credit Card Balances: $3,200

AI Response
- Total Assets: $644,000
- Total Liabilities: $324,700
- Net Worth Summary
- Net Worth = Assets - Liabilities
- = $644,000 – $324,700 = $319,300

Interpretation
Jake and Maya are in a solid financial position with a net worth of approximately $319,000. Their largest asset is their home, followed by retirement accounts and a healthy emergency fund. They have also started investing through a taxable brokerage account, which provides flexibility outside of retirement planning. Their financial foundation includes some liquidity (checking and savings) and long-term growth potential (401(k) and Roth IRA). Overall, their assets reflect

responsible financial habits and a mix of short-, medium-, and long-term planning.

On the liability side, they carry a typical mortgage balance, a small student loan, a car loan, and manageable credit card debt. The good news is that their debts are well below their asset base, and none appear dangerously high relative to their income or savings. Their net worth has room to grow quickly if they continue investing consistently and avoid adding new high-interest debt.

Savings and Emergency Fund Sample Prompts

- "Based on my average monthly living expenses of $[X], calculate how much I should aim to keep in an emergency fund to cover 3–6 months of expenses. Include both a minimum and an ideal savings target."
- "Help me build a monthly savings plan to reach a $15,000 emergency fund within the next 12 months. I can save $[X] per month right now. If I am behind, suggest ways to close the gap."
- "Where is the best place to keep my emergency savings so that it earns some interest but is still easy to access if needed? Compare options like high-yield savings accounts, money market funds, and short-term certificates of deposit (CDs), and explain the trade-offs for liquidity, safety, and yield."
- "I have $3,000 saved and want to grow it to $10,000 in two years. What is a realistic monthly savings goal?"
- "I have $[X] saved in my emergency fund, and my current monthly expenses are $[Y]. If I lose my job or have

no income, estimate how many months this fund would last. Include a basic spending breakdown and areas where I could cut back in an emergency."

- "What percentage of my total savings should be allocated to an emergency fund compared to other priorities like investing, saving for a down payment, or short-term purchases? I want to stay prepared without over-allocating to low-return accounts."

Example Prompt with Output and Interpretation

Prompt
"I have $3,000 saved and want to grow it to $10,000 in two years. What is a realistic monthly savings goal?"

AI Response
To grow your savings from $3,000 to $10,000 in two years, you need to save an additional $7,000. Divide that $7,000 by 24 months, and you get a base monthly savings goal of about $291.67.

If you plan to keep your money in a high-yield savings account earning interest (let's assume 4% annual percentage yield (APY)[18] compounded monthly), you can reduce the required monthly savings slightly. Accounting for interest, you'd need to save around $280 per month to reach $10,000 in two years.

---

18 Annual percentage yield (APY) shows how much you'll earn from an account in one year, including the effects of compounding. A higher APY means your money grows faster.

> ### Interpretation
>
> If you already have $3,000 saved and want to reach $10,000 in two years, you'll need to save around $280 to $290 per month, depending on the interest rate of your account. Saving a little over $9 a day will help you achieve this goal, especially if you use a high-yield account that pays interest.

Progress and Direction

Once you take the time to understand your finances, you will have a clearer picture of where you stand. You will know what's coming in, what's going out, what you owe, and what you own. Moreover, you'll have a personal balance sheet and income statement that reflect your real financial life. That is powerful. It is the kind of awareness that turns vague goals into actual plans. And the best part? AI can help you maintain that clarity by running the numbers, sorting your transactions, estimating your cash flow, and organizing your debt so you can spend less time on spreadsheets and more time making real progress.

Remember, this is not about perfection but direction. You don't need to have everything figured out right now, but you do need to be honest with yourself and keep moving forward. Knowing your financial starting point makes every decision that follows grounded and more intentional. With AI as your assistant and a clear snapshot in front of you, you are not just hoping things will improve; you are building a system that ensures they do.

CHAPTER 6

RISK AND RISK TOLERANCE

"Volatility is the price of admission. The prize inside are superior long-term returns. You have to pay the price to get the returns."
—*Morgan Housel*

Risk is an unavoidable part of investing. Whether it involves stocks, real estate, or your own business, things do not always go as planned. However, risk isn't something to avoid but something to understand. The more clearly you can define the risks you are taking, the easier it becomes to stick to your plan, make better choices when markets sell off, and stay on track toward your goals. In this chapter, we will break down what risk really means, how to think about it in a personal and practical manner, and how AI can help you evaluate your risk tolerance and navigate it more intelligently over time.

In finance, risk typically refers to the chance that an investment's actual return will differ from its expected return. This can mean either losing money or just not growing it fast enough to meet your goals. No investment is risk-free—not even cash. If your savings are not keeping up with inflation, you are actually losing purchasing power over time. Therefore, the question isn't whether to take risks but how to take the right kind of risks for you.

The relationship between risk and reward is at the heart of investing. Higher-return investments usually come with higher volatility, which means bigger swings in value. This is why stocks tend to return more than bonds over the long run and why investing in startups (or cryptocurrencies) can be so volatile. To grow wealth, you often have to stomach some short-term uncertainty. Trying to avoid all risk can result in underperformance and falling short of your financial goals.

Types of Risk Every Investor Should Know

Before diving into your own risk tolerance, it is helpful to understand some of the different types of risk:

- Market Risk: This refers to the risk that the entire market or a segment of it declines.
- Interest Rate Risk: If rates go up (or down), the value of existing bonds usually falls (or rises). This applies to bonds and is sometimes referred to as price risk.
- Inflation Risk: This refers to the chance that your returns do not outpace inflation.
- Credit Risk: This refers to the risk that a borrower will default. It is mainly relevant for bonds and lending.
- Liquidity Risk: This refers to the risk of not being able to sell an investment quickly at fair value.
- Concentration Risk: This refers to having too much in one asset, sector, or region.
- Behavioral Risk: This refers to the risk of making poor decisions, usually driven by emotions such as fear or greed, especially during volatile periods.

You do not need to memorize all of these, and not every investment carries every type of risk. However, being aware of them helps you better evaluate what you are really signing up for with each investment.

How Much Risk Can You Live With?

Risk tolerance is your personal comfort level with uncertainty and potential loss. It is not just about how much you think you can handle, but also about how you actually respond when markets become volatile. Some people can watch their portfolio drop by 20% and barely blink, while others feel stressed when it declines by 5%. There is no right or wrong answer here. However, if you invest in a way that does not match your true tolerance, you are more likely to panic-sell during a downturn, which is one of the most damaging financial mistakes you can make as a long-term investor.

Your risk tolerance is shaped by many factors, including the following:
- Your age and time horizon
- Your income and job security
- Your personality and past experiences with money
- Your goals and what you are investing in

This is why two people with the same salary and investment timeline can have very different portfolios. One might primarily own stocks, whereas the other might prefer a conservative mix of bonds and cash. What matters is that the portfolio fits you.

Another helpful concept to understand is risk capacity, which refers to how much risk you can afford to take based on your financial situation. Someone young with a stable job and decades to invest may have high risk capacity, but if they lose sleep over every market dip, they may want a more balanced approach. Conversely, a retiree with plenty of money saved might tolerate risk emotionally, but should not invest aggressively because they may need to preserve capital. The best investment strategy strikes a balance between what you can afford to lose and what you can emotionally handle without second-guessing your plan.

Our emotional responses to risk are where things get real. It is one thing to say that you are okay with volatility when the market is rising, but quite another to watch your 401(k) drop by tens of thousands of dollars and remain calm. Many investors sabotage themselves by reacting emotionally to short-term market moves. They chase hot trends, panic when prices fall, and bail out of good strategies at the worst times. Behavioral finance consistently demonstrates that the biggest threat to your portfolio is not the market but your own behavior. When it comes to investing, emotional discipline can be more important than technical expertise at times.

Smarter Risk Management with AI

AI is changing the game when it comes to understanding and managing risk—not by replacing human judgment but by sharpening it. Instead of guessing how much risk you can handle based on a one-time quiz, AI can analyze how you actually behave with your investments over time. It can help you examine your past decisions, reactions to market movements, and portfolio choices to build a more accurate picture of your true risk profile. This means less guesswork and more alignment between your investment plan and your personality.

Furthermore, AI can run simulations that illustrate how your portfolio might perform in different scenarios (e.g., recessions, bear markets, or bull markets). It can help you visualize both the potential gains and the potential drawdowns over time, which is incredibly useful for setting expectations and avoiding emotional decision-making. If you are debating between different strategies, such as a conservative 60% stocks/40% bonds portfolio or a more aggressive all-stock approach, AI can walk you through the trade-offs side by side. You can see not just the expected returns but also the downside risk, volatility, and likelihood of reaching your goals.

Furthermore, you can also prompt AI directly, which is where the real power starts to show. Ask questions like "How would my portfolio have performed in 2008?" or "What is the impact on my retirement if the market drops 20% next year?" AI can provide answers with charts, tables, timelines, and probabilities to help you make more informed decisions. It can even offer personalized nudges based on your age, goals, and investment behavior, reminding you to rebalance, increase savings, or stay the course when emotions are high. It is about taking the right kind of risk and sticking with your plan.

Prompts That Help You Think More Clearly About Risk

- "Simulate a 90% stocks/10% bonds portfolio over the past 20 years. What was the worst year and the average annual return?"
- "How would a 70% stocks/30% bonds portfolio have performed during the 2008 financial crisis?"

77

- "Compare the downside risk of VTI versus QQQ in terms of maximum drawdown and volatility."[19]
- "If I reduce my stock exposure by 10%, how does that impact expected returns and risk over a 30-year period?"

These are just starting points. You can go deeper with follow-up questions, upload your own portfolio, or ask AI to walk you through different market scenarios.

Forecasting Versus Simulating

As intelligent as AI is, it is not a fortune teller. It will not tell you what the S&P 500 will do next month or whether interest rates will rise next quarter. However, it can help you understand the range of possible outcomes based on history, patterns, and reasonable assumptions. That alone can be incredibly valuable. Instead of trying to guess the future, you are utilizing data to prepare for it, which is a much better strategy for managing investment risk.

AI can assist with both forecasting and simulating, and it's important to know the difference. Forecasting involves projecting what might happen over time using factors like average returns, expected volatility, and how long you plan to stay invested. It's great for long-term planning—like asking, "What could my portfolio grow to in 20 years if I earn 6% annually?" Conversely, simulations test your portfolio under pressure. You

---

19   VTI is the Vanguard Total Stock Market ETF. It gives you exposure to almost the entire US stock market, including large, mid, and small companies. QQQ is the Invesco Nasdaq-100 ETF. It is more concentrated in information technology and growth-oriented stocks, holding many of the biggest names on the NASDAQ.

can model a 2008-style crash, a prolonged bear market, or a rising interest rate environment to see how your investments might hold up. It is similar to stress-testing your financial plan before the storm hits.

Forecasting and simulating both have their place, and the goal is not perfection but perspective. Although forecasts and simulations aren't exact, they help set expectations and reduce surprises. This is a big deal when you are trying to stay committed to a plan during uncertain times. AI can help shift your mindset from "What will happen?" to "What could happen, and am I prepared for it?" This shift is one of the most powerful ways to reduce emotional decision-making and build investing confidence.

Every Choice Comes with a Trade-Off

Every investing decision comes with trade-offs, and there is no way around it. Want higher long-term growth? That usually means taking on more volatility with stocks. Want more stability? That often means leaning into bonds or cash, which also typically come with lower expected returns. Even holding a large cash balance, which feels safe on the surface, has its own hidden cost: inflation slowly eroding your purchasing power. There is no free lunch in investing, and you are typically giving something up to gain something else. The real question is: are you making trade-offs that align with your personality and your goals?

This is where AI can really help you think clearly. It will not sugarcoat the decisions but will instead show you the implications in black and white. You can ask questions like "What's the expected difference in return if I go 100% stocks versus a 70% stocks/30% bonds mix?" or "How could my portfolio perform if the US dollar weakens and I have more international exposure?" These comparisons are powerful, allowing you to see not just potential gains but also the kind of downside you'd need to endure. This can be a crucial missing piece in traditional advice. AI can even assist with decision timing by modeling scenarios like "Should I invest now or wait six months with this $10,000?" The goal is not to find a perfect answer but to understand the risks and rewards of each option.

Your Plan Should Change

Here's the thing: your investment plan should not be static. As your life evolves, your income, goals, and risk tolerance will shift as well. For instance, you may get married, start a business, or decide to retire early. AI can help you make thoughtful adjustments as you go. You can ask, "Based on my age and retirement timeline, should I start shifting more toward bonds?" or "How can I reduce my portfolio's volatility without sacrificing too much return?" If your portfolio is too concentrated in one sector or company, AI can flag that and help you diversify intelligently. It is like having a financial coach that stays updated in real-time.

Besides, AI is excellent at helping you stick with your plan when emotions start creeping in. If the market drops significantly, you can ask, "Remind me why I shouldn't sell right now," and it will walk you through the data, history, and likely outcomes of acting on fear. Moreover, it can show you what happened in similar market downturns in the past, what recoveries looked like, and how those who stayed invested typically came out ahead. Sometimes, we just need a voice of reason, and AI can be that steady, rational voice when it's hardest to hear your own. The goal is not to eliminate all risk or emotion but to take smart risks, manage them thoughtfully, and stay on course with a plan that adjusts as you do.

Manage Risk, Don't Avoid It

Risk is not the enemy; it is a part of investing. The key is knowing your own tolerance for uncertainty, building a portfolio that fits your goals and comfort level, and staying disciplined. AI can support you in that process by testing different assumptions and keeping your plan anchored in data instead of emotion. The investors who succeed are not the ones who avoid risk but those who understand it, manage it well, and remain committed.

Example Prompt with Output and Interpretation

Prompt
"Create a risk tolerance questionnaire for an investor to complete and assess their risk tolerance."

AI Response
Below is a complete risk tolerance questionnaire for investors.

Risk Tolerance Questionnaire
Instructions: Answer each question honestly based on how you actually feel and behave, not how you think you should answer. Use your gut.

1. What's your investment time horizon?
   A. Less than 3 years – 1 point
   B. 3 to 5 years – 2 points
   C. 6 to 10 years – 3 points
   D. More than 10 years – 4 points
2. How would you feel if your portfolio dropped 20% in a single year?
   A. I'd panic and want to sell – 1 point
   B. I'd be concerned but stay invested – 2 points
   C. I'd see it as a buying opportunity – 3 points
   D. I'd stay calm and trust the long-term plan – 4 points
3. How familiar are you with investing concepts like diversification, volatility, and compounding?
   A. Not familiar – 1 point
   B. Somewhat familiar – 2 points
   C. Fairly knowledgeable – 3 points
   D. Very comfortable and experienced – 4 points
4. What's more important to you right now?
   A. Avoiding loss – 1 point
   B. Earning some return without too much risk – 2 points
   C. Growing my money steadily over time – 3 points
   D. Maximizing returns, even if it means short-term losses – 4 points
5. If an investment you made dropped 10% right after you bought it, what would you do?
   A. Sell and avoid further loss – 1 point
   B. Wait to see what happens – 2 points
   C. Hold and review the fundamentals – 3 points
   D. Buy more – 4 points

6. How stable is your income and job situation?
   A. Very unstable – 1 point
   B. Somewhat stable – 2 points
   C. Mostly stable – 3 points
   D. Very stable – 4 points
7. Have you ever invested through a market downturn (e.g., 2008, 2020)?
   A. No – 1 point
   B. Yes, but I pulled out – 2 points
   C. Yes, and I stayed invested – 3 points
   D. Yes, and I invested more – 4 points

Scoring Guide
- 7–12 points: Very conservative
- 13–17 points: Moderate
- 18–22 points: Growth-oriented
- 23–28 points: Aggressive

Interpretation

Your score provides a rough sense of your risk tolerance—not just what you're capable of handling but also how you're wired to react when the market becomes volatile. If you scored on the lower end, it indicates that you likely prefer stability, smaller swings, and peace of mind over chasing high returns. There is nothing wrong with this, especially if your financial goals are near-term or your life situation demands more predictability.

If your score is higher, you are probably comfortable with short-term ups and downs in exchange for greater long-term growth. You are also likely okay riding out the dips and staying focused on the big picture.

There is no right or wrong here; the goal is for you to build a portfolio that aligns with your comfort level so you do not make emotional decisions when markets become volatile. Reaching your financial goals includes building something that you can stick with in all market conditions.

Example Prompt with Output and Interpretation

Prompt
"How can I use my risk tolerance score to form a suggested asset allocation?"

AI Response
You can use a risk tolerance score to guide a suggested asset allocation by mapping the investor's comfort with risk to a mix of stocks (equities), bonds (fixed income), and sometimes cash or alternatives. Here's how to approach it practically:

Step-by-Step: From Score to Allocation
The following table uses the scoring buckets from your quiz:

Score Range	Risk Profile	Suggested Allocation (Stocks/Bonds)
7–12	Very conservative	20% stocks/80% bonds
13–17	Moderate	40% stocks/60% bonds

Score Range	Risk Profile	Suggested Allocation (Stocks/Bonds)
18–22	Growth-oriented	60–70% stocks/30–40% bonds
23–28	Aggressive	80–90% stocks/10–20% bonds

You can adjust the percentages based on age, financial goals, and investment timeline.

How to Use This Score in Practice

- Start with the quiz score to get a general sense of how aggressive or conservative someone should be.
- Adjust based on time horizon. Someone may score "moderate," but if they won't need the money for 30 years, a growth-leaning allocation (like 70% stocks/30% bonds) might still be appropriate.
- Layer in goals and income stability. If they are nearing retirement or have an unstable job, even a high scorer might want more bonds for stability.
- Check for emotional fit. If someone claims they can handle 80% in stocks but panicked in 2008 or 2020, dial it back to something they can actually stick with.

Interpretation

You want your portfolio to match your attitude toward risk so that you will not panic-sell when (not if) markets become volatile. Your risk tolerance score provides a helpful way to explain why a 70% stocks/30% bonds or 60% stocks/40% bonds allocation makes sense. AI can help you identify a portfolio mix that aligns with how you answered your risk tolerance questionnaire. Ultimately, the best portfolio is one you can live with.

Example Prompt with Output and Interpretation

Prompt

"What is a typical asset allocation for a moderate-risk profile individual who has student loans and is new to investing?"

AI Response

For a moderate-risk investor who is new to investing and has student loans, a typical asset allocation might look as follows:

Suggested Asset Allocation

Asset Class	Allocation
Stocks (equities)	60%
Bonds (fixed income)	35%
Cash/short-term	5%

Breakdown
- 60% Stocks: This allocation provides growth potential but with less volatility than an aggressive (80–90%) equity portfolio. A mix of US total market, international, and perhaps a small slice of sector or dividend funds can work well.

- 35% Bonds: This adds stability and helps reduce the emotional rollercoaster when markets swing. You could use a total bond market fund or a target-date fund[20] if you prefer something simple.
- 5% Cash: A small buffer for emergencies or near-term expenses, especially important if you are balancing loan payments with investing.

Interpretation

If you are new to investing and still paying off student loans, you don't need to take on excessive risk to get started. A 60% stocks/40% bonds setup allows you to grow your money while keeping the ride manageable. The key early on is building the habit, staying consistent, and not letting short-term swings throw you off your plan. You can always increase your risk exposure later as you become more comfortable with investing. Prompts like this can be customized for anyone to describe their risk profile, current situation, available resources, and current investments, and they can be updated as the person's situation changes over time.

Last Thing About Risk

Even though you cannot avoid risk, that does not mean it has to make you uncomfortable. The real danger isn't the market itself; it's reacting to it in ways that derail your long-term plan.

---

20 A target date mutual fund is a diversified investment that automatically adjusts its mix of stocks and bonds based on a specific retirement year. It starts out more aggressive when you are far from retirement and gradually becomes more conservative as the target date approaches.

By understanding the different types of risk, knowing your personal tolerance and capacity, and acknowledging how emotions can cloud judgment, you are already ahead of most investors. It's not about finding a path with no risk but about choosing risks that align with your goals, timeline, and temperament.

The good news is that you don't have to navigate this journey alone. AI functions as a smart, data-driven partner that helps you evaluate trade-offs, stress-test your portfolio, and adjust your strategy without getting swept up in fear or hype. It does not eliminate risk, but it can help you better understand it. That's the real advantage, because the investor who understands their risks and adheres to their plan is the one most likely to reach their goals.

CHAPTER 7

POPULAR INVESTMENT ACCOUNTS AND ASSET LOCATION

"It's not what you earn, it's what you keep."
—Unknown

When it comes to investing, choosing the right account type is just as important as selecting the right investments. Most people are familiar with basic accounts like a 401(k) or Roth IRA, but each account type serves a different purpose. Some offer tax breaks now, while others reward you later. Therefore, understanding how each account works can help you build a strategy that not only grows your money but also keeps more of it in your pocket over time.

Account Types by Tax Treatment

Popular investment accounts fall into three broad categories: tax-deferred (like traditional 401(k)s and IRAs), tax-free (like

Roth IRAs and Roth 401(k)s), and taxable brokerage accounts. Tax-deferred accounts can provide an immediate tax break but come with taxes due later. Roth accounts do not offer an upfront deduction, but they allow your investments to grow and be withdrawn tax-free in retirement. Taxable accounts provide the most flexibility—you can invest and withdraw when you want—but gains and income may be taxed each year.

Comparison of Investment Account Types

Account Type	Examples	Tax Treatment	Best For	Considerations
Tax-deferred	Traditional 401(k), traditional IRA	Contributions may be tax-deductible; growth is tax-deferred; taxed on withdrawal	Lowering taxable income now; long-term growth	Required minimum distributions; taxed in retirement
Tax-free	Roth IRA, Roth 401(k)	Contributions made with after-tax dollars; growth and withdrawals are tax-free under qualifying conditions, such as after age 59½	Younger investors; long-term tax-free growth	No tax deduction now; income limits may apply (Roth IRA)

Account Type	Examples	Tax Treatment	Best For	Considerations
Taxable	Brokerage account	No tax advantages; pay taxes on dividends, interest, and realized gains	Flexibility; access anytime	No contribution limits; less tax-efficient if actively trading

What is Asset Location?

This is where asset location comes into play. Asset allocation refers to what you own, while asset location refers to where you own it. Think of it like organizing a toolbox; you want to place the right tools in the right compartments. When you think about asset location, the goal is to match the right type of investment with the right type of account. Each account has different tax rules, and you can use that to your advantage. Below is a simple framework:

- Tax-Deferred Accounts (401(k), traditional IRA): These are best for investments that generate a lot of taxable income, like bonds or REITs. You do not pay taxes while the money grows, but you will when you withdraw it.
- Roth Accounts (Roth IRA, Roth 401(k)): These are best for assets with strong growth potential, such as stock funds or anything you expect to multiply over time. All the growth and withdrawals are tax-free later, which makes the Roth a great place for investments you want to maximize tax-free growth.
- Taxable Brokerage Accounts: These are best suited for tax-efficient investments that generate little taxable income, like broad index funds, ETFs, or individual stocks

you plan to hold for a while. They also work well for investments you may sell sooner, since gains held over a year qualify for the lower long-term capital gains tax rate.

The goal is to use each account's tax features to your advantage while keeping your overall portfolio aligned with your risk tolerance and goals. A thoughtful asset location strategy can enhance your after-tax returns over time without taking on more risk. It's one of those behind-the-scenes moves that can quietly make a significant difference.

Example Prompt with Output and Interpretation

Prompt
"I am new to investing and looking to open my first brokerage account. Which platforms are best for beginners who want low fees, easy-to-use tools, and access to a wide range of investment options? Please compare a few top choices and explain the pros and cons of each."

AI Response
Best Brokerage Platforms for Beginners: A Comparison
If you are new to investing and looking for your first brokerage account, the best platforms will offer low fees, intuitive interfaces, and access to a variety of investment options, such as stocks, ETFs, and retirement accounts. Below are a few top choices for beginners, along with their pros and cons.

Fidelity

Pros:

- $0 commission on stocks and ETFs
- Strong customer service and educational tools
- Access to a wide range of investment options (including mutual funds with no minimums)
- Cash management and high-yield savings features
- Well-regarded mobile and desktop platforms

Cons:

- Research tools can feel overwhelming at first
- Fractional share[21] trading is available, but it is not as streamlined as some newer apps

Best for:

- Beginners who want long-term flexibility and strong support

Charles Schwab

Pros:

- $0 commissions on stocks, ETFs, and options
- Excellent reputation and customer service
- Offers fractional shares through "Stock Slices"
- Great for retirement accounts (IRAs, Roth IRAs)
- Access to the Schwab Intelligent Portfolios robo-advisor

---

21 Fractional shares let you buy a portion of a stock or ETF instead of a full share. They make it easier to invest small amounts regularly.

Cons:

- Interface is more traditional and slightly less modern than some competitors
- The mobile app is functional but less sleek than Robinhood or SoFi[22]

Best for:

- Investors who want full-service features with low costs

Vanguard

Pros:

- Strong focus on long-term, low-cost investing
- Access to some of the most respected mutual funds and ETFs in the world
- Ideal for retirement-focused investors
- Excellent reputation for putting investors first

Cons:

- Fewer real-time trading tools; geared more toward buy-and-hold investors

Best for:

- Long-term investors who want to build a passive, low-cost portfolio

---

22 Robinhood and SoFi are online investing platforms that make it easy for individuals to buy investments such as stocks and ETFs with no account minimums. They're designed for convenience, but ease of use should not replace doing your homework before investing.

SoFi Invest

Pros:

- $0 commissions on stocks and ETFs
- Clean, modern interface—very beginner-friendly
- Offers both active investing and robo-advisor options
- Free access to financial planners for members
- Offers banking and loan products

Cons:

- Limited research and analytical tools compared to larger brokers
- Investment selection is more basic

Best for:

- New investors who want a simple, all-in-one money app

Robinhood

Pros:

- $0 commissions
- Extremely easy-to-use mobile app
- Offers fractional shares and crypto trading
- Fast sign-up and account funding

Cons:

- Limited investor education and research tools
- History of outages and controversial practices (e.g., order flow payment)

Best for:

- Beginners who want a very simple, mobile-first investing experience, but only for small dollar amounts or learning

Summary Table

Platform	Strengths	Cautions	Best For
Fidelity	Full-featured, great service	Can feel complex	Long-term, supported investing
Schwab	Balanced and reliable	Interface less modern	All-around starter choice
Vanguard	Best for passive investing	Clunky interface	Retirement and long-term focus
SoFi	User-friendly and all-in-one	Limited research tools	Simple first-time investing
Robinhood	Extremely easy to start with	Limited support and features	Learning, experimenting

For most beginners, Fidelity and Schwab strike the best balance of cost, tools, support, and investment variety. If your focus is retirement or passive investing, Vanguard is ideal. If you prefer a simpler app-based experience, SoFi is a safe place to start. Robinhood can be fun to explore, but it should be approached cautiously.

Interpretation

If you are just getting started, platforms like Fidelity, Schwab, and Vanguard can be great choices because they offer low fees, strong support, and a wide range of investment options. SoFi is simple and beginner-friendly, especially if you want everything in one app. Robinhood makes it easy to get started, but it comes with fewer tools and less support, making it better suited for learning. The best platform is the one you feel comfortable using and can grow with over time.

Example Prompt with Output and Interpretation

Prompt

"I have approximately $500 per month to invest. I want to open and contribute to a Roth IRA, a 401(k) through my job (with a match), and a taxable brokerage account. How should I prioritize which accounts to fund first, and what types of investments make the most sense in each one based on taxes, growth potential, and flexibility? I'm in my early 30s, want to invest for the long term, and can handle some volatility. Please give me a suggested plan for:

- how to split the $500 across the three accounts;
- what types of investments (e.g., index funds, REITs, and bonds) to hold in each account; and
- why this setup makes sense: for tax efficiency and long-term growth."

AI Response

How to Split the $500 Across the Three Accounts

With limited funds, start with the account that provides you with the most immediate benefit:

- 401(k): Contribute $125 per month (or whatever amount gets you the full employer match). That is free money, and you do not want to miss out on it.
- Roth IRA: Contribute $250 per month if you're eligible based on income. This allows for tax-free growth and flexibility later in life.
- Taxable Account: Contribute $125 per month with whatever is left. This account provides liquidity and has no contribution limits, which is helpful for goals before retirement.

You can always adjust these amounts over time, but this structure provides you with a solid foundation while balancing tax benefits and flexibility.

What Investments to Hold in Each Account

Here's a smart way to think about asset location based on tax efficiency and growth potential:

- 401(k): Hold bonds, REITs, and target-date or balanced funds. These generate regular income that would be taxed annually in a regular account, but in a 401(k), it grows tax-deferred.
- Roth IRA: Use this for higher-growth assets like total market or small-cap stock index funds. Since Roth growth is tax-free, you want your highest-upside investments here.

- Taxable Brokerage Account: Stick to tax-efficient index ETFs (like VTI, SCHB, or VXUS).[23] These have low turnover and generate fewer taxable events. This is also where you might keep cash for shorter-term goals.

Why This Setup Makes Sense

This approach maximizes each account's unique strengths. The 401(k) lowers your taxable income now and is great for less tax-efficient investments. The Roth IRA grows tax-free forever, so you want to load it up with assets that can really compound over decades. The taxable account provides flexibility for activities like buying a house, starting a business, or retiring early—without early withdrawal penalties.

Interpretation

With a modest monthly amount to invest, the key is being intentional. This setup offers a balanced mix of benefits: you earn the match from your employer, build a tax-free growth engine with your Roth IRA, and give yourself flexibility with a taxable account.

---

23 VXUS is Vanguard's Total International Stock ETF, which holds non-US equities across developed and emerging international markets. VTI and SCHB, defined earlier, focus on the US stock market.

Example Prompt with Output and Interpretation

Prompt

"What is the best way for a person with a full-time job and an additional source of income to contribute as much as possible to tax-advantaged accounts?"

AI Response

Great question—this is a powerful tax and wealth-building opportunity that many high-achieving professionals overlook or underuse. If you have a full-time job with access to a 401(k) and an additional income stream (as a sole proprietor or Limited Liability Company (LLC)), you can legally stack multiple tax-advantaged accounts; you just have to understand how the contribution limits work.

Strategy Overview: Maximize All Available Buckets

1. Max Out Your Workplace 401(k):
   o Limit (2025): $23,000 employee deferral ($30,500 if 50+)
   o Employer match is separate and doesn't reduce your limit
   o Tip: Always take advantage of the full match—it's free money
2. Contribute to an IRA (Traditional or Roth):
   o Limit: $7,000 ($8,000 if age 50+)
   o Roth IRA is subject to income limits, but a Backdoor Roth may be possible if you're over the income threshold

o   Traditional IRA may be nondeductible if you're covered by a 401(k) and earn too much, but it can still be used for a Backdoor Roth

3. Open a Solo 401(k) for Your Additional Income Stream:

o   Even though you've already maxed your employee deferral at your full-time job, you can still contribute to a Solo 401(k) as the employer

o   What you can still contribute: Up to 25% of net self-employment income (after subtracting self-employment tax)

o   Maximum total Solo 401(k) contributions (2025): $69,000 ($76,500 if age 50+) minus what you already contributed as an employee at your day job; example:

   •   You earn $200,000 at your job and max out your $23,000 employee deferral

   •   Your additional income stream earns $80,000 net (after expenses)

   •   You may be able to contribute approximately $15,000–$18,000 more as the employer into your Solo 401(k), depending on your net earnings and self-employment tax

Pro tip: Use an accountant or Solo 401(k) calculator to determine the exact employer amount. Many providers like Fidelity, Vanguard, or E*TRADE offer low-cost Solo 401(k)s.

4. Use an HSA If Eligible:
   - If you have a high-deductible health plan (HDHP) from your full-time job:
     o Contribute up to $4,300 (individual) or $8,600 (family) in 2025 (+$1,000 catch-up if 55+)
     o The triple tax benefit makes this one of the best stealth retirement tools available
5. Invest the Overflow in a Taxable Brokerage Account:
   - No tax deferral, but unlimited contributions
   - Long-term capital gains and qualified dividends are taxed at favorable rates
   - This can serve as a "bridge" account if you plan to retire early before age 59½

Smart Moves to Maximize Efficiency

Account Type	Tax Treatment	Maximize If…
401(k) (Day Job)	Pre-tax or Roth	Your employer offers good funds and a match.
Roth IRA/backdoor Roth	Tax-free growth	You're under the income limit or know how to convert.
Solo 401(k)	Pre-tax or Roth	Your additional income source generates meaningful income.

Account Type	Tax Treatment	Maximize If...
HSA	Triple tax-advantaged	You have an HDHP.
Brokerage account	Taxable	You're maxing out everything else.

Interpretation

If you have a full-time job and an additional income stream, you're in a great position to supercharge your retirement savings using multiple tax-advantaged accounts. Start by maxing out your workplace 401(k), which has a limit of $23,000 for 2025, plus any employer match. If your job offers an HSA and you're on a high-deductible health plan, that's another powerful tool. From there, contribute to a Roth IRA if you're eligible or use a backdoor Roth if your income is too high. That adds $7,000 in tax-free growth potential.

However, here's where the additional income source really gives you an edge: you can open a Solo 401(k) and contribute more as the employer. Even though you've already used up your employee deferral at your main job, you can still put away up to 25% of your side business profits as an employer contribution—often another $15,000–$20,000 or more, depending on how much you earn. Stack all of that together, and you could be putting over $60,000 a year into tax-favored accounts. The big picture takeaway is that having both a primary and an additional source of income doesn't just increase your income; it also opens the door to a much more aggressive savings strategy. If you're serious about building wealth and reducing your tax bill, learning how to use every available account to your advantage is a game-changer.

Asset Location Scenario

Let's revisit asset location. Below is a sample scenario showing how a couple might spread their investments across different accounts:

- Risk Tolerance: Moderate-to-growth-oriented
- Total Combined Investment Portfolio: $300,000
- Target Allocation: 70% stocks/30% bonds, currently $210,000 in stocks and $90,000 in bonds

Account Breakdown and Asset Location

Account	Total Value	Holdings
401(k)s	$120,000	$90,000 in bonds, $30,000 in US large-cap index funds
Roth IRAs	$80,000	$80,000 in stock index funds (small-cap, international stock index funds)
Taxable brokerage	$100,000	$100,000 in low-yield, tax-efficient stock index funds[24]

---

24 ETFs are often more tax-friendly than mutual funds. When investors sell shares of an ETF, the fund does not usually have to sell its own investments, which helps avoid triggering capital gains. Mutual funds, on the other hand, may have to sell investments to meet redemptions, which can create taxable gains for all investors in the fund.

Total Portfolio Breakdown (by Asset Type):

- Stocks ($210,000 total):
    - o $30,000 in 401(k)s
    - o $80,000 in Roth IRAs
    - o $100,000 in taxable
- Bonds ($90,000 total):
    - o   All $90,000 in 401(k)s

This setup keeps the couple's 70% stocks/30% bonds allocation intact, but it does it in a way that makes their money work harder. Bonds sit in the 401(k)s, where their taxable interest does not create a tax bill. Growth stocks go in the Roth IRAs, where compounding happens tax-free. The taxable account holds low-yielding, efficient ETFs to minimize taxes and maintain portfolio flexibility, with investments that can be accessed before retirement if desired.

For AI to help with asset location, you should share the following information with it:

- Account Types: What types of accounts do you have? (e.g., traditional IRA, Roth IRA, 401(k), and brokerage).
- Account Balances: How much is in each account?
- Asset Allocation: What is your target mix of stocks, bonds, and other assets?
- Investment Preferences: Are there specific funds or holdings you are using or want to use?
- Time Horizon: When do you plan to use the money in each account?
- Tax Bracket: What's your current marginal tax rate (and projected future rate if known)?
- Income Needs: Are you drawing income from any accounts now?
- State of Residence: For state tax considerations.

- Capital Gains Exposure: Any large unrealized gains in taxable accounts?

With this information, it can recommend where to place different asset types (like stocks versus bonds) to help reduce taxes and potentially boost after-tax returns.

Why All of This Matters

Asset location is one of those underrated strategies that can quietly boost your after-tax returns over time. The idea is simple: put tax-efficient investments, such as low-yielding ETFs, in taxable accounts, and tax-inefficient ones, such as bonds, in tax-advantaged accounts like a traditional IRA or 401(k). AI can help by analyzing your holdings, identifying where each investment is currently located, and suggesting a more tax-efficient placement based on your goals and time horizon. It can even run scenarios showing the potential long-term impact of different setups, helping you see whether the extra effort is worth it. Done well, this can save you a good amount in taxes without changing your overall investment mix. The downside, however, is that it can make your portfolio a little harder to manage and might reduce your flexibility if you ever need to access funds from a specific account without impacting your asset allocation. If you do not optimize for asset location, you will still be fine—steady saving and smart investing matter most. It is simply a way to keep more of what you earn, a quiet boost rather than a requirement.

CHAPTER 8

ASSETS TO OWN

"Know what you own and know why you own it."
—*Peter Lynch*

When building an investment portfolio, it is helpful to understand the traditional major asset classes, namely, stocks, bonds, cash and cash equivalents, real estate, and alternatives, each of which plays a different role and carries its own set of risks, return potential, and tax considerations. Stocks, for example, represent ownership in companies and offer long-term growth potential, while bonds are debt instruments that provide more stable, predictable income. Cash and cash equivalents, such as money market funds or CDs, are safe and liquid, but investors pay for that security with very low returns. Real estate can provide income and capital appreciation, and alternatives such as commodities, hedge funds, or private equity offer diversification and potentially uncorrelated returns.

What Most Investors Invest In

Despite the full menu of asset classes available, most individual investors primarily stick with just two: stocks and bonds. There is nothing inherently wrong with that—after all, stocks and bonds have historically formed the core of most portfolios, and together they offer a good mix of growth and stability. However, relying solely on these two can occasionally leave a portfolio exposed to more risk than necessary, especially if the investor does not rebalance or diversify across sectors and geographies. Additionally, it also limits the potential benefits that other asset classes can bring, particularly in environments where traditional stock/bond portfolios may struggle.

Real estate and alternatives are often overlooked, at times because they are less accessible or seem more complex. However, owning rental property, investing in REITs, or including something like commodities can add a layer of diversification that helps cushion a portfolio during inflationary periods or when markets are volatile. Besides, these assets can also behave differently from stocks and bonds, providing some balance when traditional assets move in sync. The same goes for holding some cash—not necessarily as an investment for growth but as dry powder for opportunities or to weather emergencies without selling long-term holdings.

Ultimately, most people do not need exposure to all five asset classes at once, but understanding what each offers can lead to smarter, more intentional investing. If you are just starting, building a strong foundation with stocks and bonds makes sense. However, as your portfolio grows or your goals become more specific, it is worth revisiting your mix and considering whether other asset classes could help you better manage risk, generate income, or meet long-term objectives more efficiently.

Asset allocation is one of the most important decisions you will make, and expanding your view beyond just stocks and bonds can pay off in the long run.

Example Prompt with Output and Interpretation

Prompt

"When investing, should I focus on picking individual stocks and bonds or focus on funds? If picking stocks and bonds is recommended, what should I focus on?"

AI Output

For most investors, especially those looking for simplicity, diversification, and long-term performance, focusing on funds such as ETFs and mutual funds is usually the smarter and more efficient approach. Funds offer built-in diversification, professional management (for active funds), and low costs (for index funds). Thus, they allow you to gain exposure to entire asset classes or market segments with a single investment, reducing the risk of being wrong about any one company or bond.

That said, if you're experienced, enjoy research, and have time to manage your portfolio actively, picking individual stocks and bonds can make sense, but you'll want to be strategic. For stocks, focus on companies with durable competitive advantages, strong balance sheets, consistent cash flow, and reasonable valuations. You should understand the business, its risks, and its growth drivers. For bonds, consider the issuer's credit quality, interest rate risk, and the bond's place in your overall asset allocation. In both cases, you should only invest in individual securities if you're willing to monitor them regularly and can tolerate the added volatility and concentration risk.

For most people, a core-satellite strategy works well: use diversified funds as your core and selectively add individual stocks or bonds if you have conviction and understand the risks.

Interpretation

For most investors, sticking with ETFs and mutual funds is the way to go. These funds are designed to provide broad exposure to markets, allowing you to own hundreds or even thousands of companies with a single investment. This means that you are not betting everything on one stock or bond, and your risk is spread out. Funds are also low-cost, easy to manage, and do not require constant research or monitoring. If you want a simple and effective way to grow your money over time, building your portfolio around quality funds can be a smart move.

Picking individual stocks or bonds might sound appealing, especially when you hear stories about people making big gains, but it is a lot harder than it looks. You need to know how to analyze a company, understand its financials, and stay on top of news that could impact its performance. Bonds add a whole other layer of complexity with credit risk, interest rates, and maturity schedules. For most people, this level of detail and attention is not realistic, and, honestly, it is not necessary. Owning a few well-diversified funds does the heavy lifting for you and keeps your portfolio on track without the stress or guesswork.

Example Prompt with Output and Interpretation

Prompt

"What are good criteria to use in selecting ETFs and mutual funds regardless of the asset class?"

AI Output

A good set of criteria to use when selecting ETFs and mutual funds, regardless of asset class, should help you identify well-constructed, low-cost, and appropriately diversified options. Below are the most important factors to consider:

Selection Criteria (Applicable to All Asset Classes)

1. Expense Ratio:
    o   Lower is better. Aim for under 0.10% for ETFs and under 0.50% for mutual funds (some international funds and alternative investment funds may have slightly higher expense ratios due to more complex management and operational costs).
    o   Fees directly reduce your returns over time.[25]

---

25 The expense ratio is the most proven predictor of future fund returns. The cheaper the fund, the better the odds of outperforming its more expensive peers. (Morningstar, How Expense Ratios and Star Ratings Predict Success, May 2010). For example, a $100,000 investment growing at 7% annually over 30 years would grow to $761,225 with no fees. With a 1% annual expense ratio, it would grow to $574,349—a loss of $186,876 (nearly 25% less) due to fees alone. With a more modest 0.30% expense ratio, the $100,000 investment would grow to approximately $699,733 over 30 years. That's about $61,492 less than if there

2. Fund Strategy:
   o Ensure the fund's goal matches your intended exposure (e.g., US small-cap value, international bonds).

3. Diversification:
   o Look for broad exposure across the target asset class.
   o Avoid overly concentrated funds unless that's your goal.

4. Tracking Error[26] (for ETFs) / Active Risk (for Mutual Funds):
   o For ETFs, ensure they closely track their benchmark.
   o For mutual funds, evaluate how consistently they beat or trail their benchmark.

5. Fund Size/Assets Under Management (AUM):
   o Avoid very small funds (under $50M), which may have higher risks of closure or low liquidity.
   o Larger funds tend to be more stable and cost-efficient.

6. Manager Tenure and Track Record:
   o For actively managed mutual funds, look for experienced managers with at least five years of performance history.

---

were no fees. Do not ignore fees, whether it is expense ratios or even AUM fees, if someone else manages your money.

26 Tracking error measures how closely a fund's performance follows its benchmark index. It's typically expressed as the standard deviation of the difference between the fund's returns and the benchmark's returns. The lower the tracking error, the more accurately the fund is replicating the index.

- o For index funds, focus more on the structure and tracking error than the manager.
7. Portfolio Turnover:
    - o Lower turnover usually means lower trading costs and higher tax efficiency.
    - o This is especially important for taxable accounts.
8. Tax Efficiency:
    - o ETFs are generally more tax-efficient due to in-kind creation/redemption.
    - o Mutual funds can distribute large capital gains—check the fund's distribution history.
9. Morningstar or Similar Ratings (Optional):
    - o Star ratings and analyst reports can be useful as a supplement, not a primary tool.
    - o Pay more attention to "Gold" or "Silver" analyst ratings than star ratings alone.
10. Fit in Your Overall Portfolio:
    - o Does it complement your current allocation?
    - o Avoid overlapping exposure unless you're doing it intentionally (e.g., tilting to factors like value or momentum).

Interpretation

When choosing ETFs or mutual funds, no matter the asset class, the goal is straightforward: look for funds that are low-cost, well-diversified, and aligned with your needs. Start with the basics, especially expense ratios. This matters more than many investors realize. Small differences in fees compound and can take a real bite out of your returns over time. Next, make sure the fund's strategy delivers the exposure you want. If you are buying a small-cap value fund, it should behave like one. Avoid funds that are overly concentrated (unless that's intentional) and confirm you're getting broad, sensible exposure within the asset class. Beyond that, focus on quality and fit. Larger funds often bring more stability and cost efficiency, while very small funds can carry added risk. For actively managed funds, the manager's track record is worth paying attention to. Finally, do not put too much weight on fund star ratings. They can be helpful as one data point, but they should never be the deciding factor. Most importantly, always step back and ask: how does this fund fit within the rest of my portfolio?

Example Prompt with Output and Interpretation

Prompt

"Using this criterion (see previous example prompt), provide the top five ETFs and mutual funds for US stocks and explain your logic."

AI Output

Below are the five top choices that provide excellent exposure to US stocks while meeting the key criteria: low cost, broad diversification, strong fund managers, and suitability for most portfolios. These are great core building blocks, regardless of whether you're just getting started or fine-tuning an existing allocation.

Type	Fund Name	Expense Ratio (%)	Key Attributes
ETF	Vanguard Total Stock Market ETF (VTI)	0.03	Covers the entire US market; massive AUM; extremely tax-efficient; strong tracking
ETF	Schwab US Broad Market ETF (SCHB)	0.03	Very similar to VTI; low cost; great for Schwab users; diversified exposure
ETF	iShares Core S&P Total US Stock Market ETF (ITOT)	0.03	S&P Total Market Index; strong liquidity; ideal for core US exposure
Mutual Fund	Fidelity Total Market Index Fund (FSKAX)	0.015	Mutual fund version of VTI; no minimums at Fidelity; great for retirement accounts
Mutual Fund	Vanguard 500 Index Fund Admiral Shares (VFIAX)	0.04	Tracks the S&P 500; solid core holding; strong long-term track record

Why These Funds Made the Cut

These funds have the following characteristics:

- Have expense ratios under 0.05%
- Offer broad diversification across sectors and market caps
- Are issued by highly reputable firms (Vanguard, Fidelity, Schwab, iShares (BlackRock)

- Have a huge AUM, ensuring stability and liquidity
- Can serve as a core equity holding in any long-term portfolio

Interpretation

With so many ETFs and mutual funds available, it is easy to feel overwhelmed when trying to pick the right one. Therefore, by focusing on a few key criteria such as low expense ratios, broad market exposure, strong fund administrators, and long-term consistency, you can quickly narrow the list to high-quality options that are built to last. The five funds highlighted here all offer diversified exposure to US stocks at a very low cost, and they come from well-established firms like Vanguard, Fidelity, Schwab, and BlackRock. Whether you are just starting or rebalancing an existing portfolio, these funds can provide a reliable foundation.

This kind of list can significantly simplify your decision-making. Instead of sorting through hundreds of overlapping or niche funds, you can focus on a few that are efficient, diversified, and easy to build around. Whether you prefer ETFs for their tax efficiency or mutual funds for their automatic investment features, you are getting the same essential exposure to the US market. It is a straightforward way to invest without overcomplicating things, and that's often the best approach. Prompts like this one are good for other investments and asset classes, not just US stocks.

Example Prompt with Output and Interpretation

Prompt

"What are popular investments for DIY investors for all asset classes that have low fees?"

AI Output

Here's a breakdown of popular, low-fee investment options for DIY investors across all five major asset classes:

Stocks

Popular low-fee investments:
- VTI (Vanguard Total Stock Market ETF)
- SCHB (Schwab US Broad Market ETF)
- ITOT (iShares Core S&P Total US Stock Market ETF)

These broad index ETFs cover thousands of US companies, have expense ratios under 0.05%, and are ideal for diversified stock exposure.

Bonds

Popular low-fee investments:
- BND (Vanguard Total Bond Market ETF)
- AGG (iShares Core US Aggregate Bond ETF)
- SCHZ (Schwab US Aggregate Bond ETF)

These funds provide exposure to a wide range of investment-grade US bonds and typically have fees of around 0.03–0.05%.

Cash and Cash Equivalents
Popular low-fee options:
- High-Yield Online Savings Accounts (e.g., Ally, Marcus, Capital One)
- Treasury Bills (purchased directly via TreasuryDirect.gov or ETFs like SPDR[27] Bloomberg 1-3 Month T-Bill ETF (BIL))
- Money Market Funds (e.g., Vanguard Federal Money Market Fund (VMFXX))

These are safe, highly liquid options—great for emergency funds or short-term needs.

Real Estate
Popular low-fee investments:
- VNQ (Vanguard Real Estate ETF)
- SCHH (Schwab US REIT ETF)
- FREL (Fidelity MSCI Real Estate ETF)[28]

These ETFs offer low-cost access to diversified real estate through publicly traded REITs, typically with expense ratios of around 0.08–0.12%.

Alternatives
Popular low-fee investments:
- GLDM (SPDR Gold MiniShares Trust): For gold exposure

---

27 You will see SPDR in many fund names because it stands for Standard & Poor's Depositary Receipts, the name for ETFs managed by State Street Global Advisors.

28 MSCI stands for Morgan Stanley Capital International, a firm known for creating widely used market indexes. When you see MSCI in a fund's name, it typically means the fund is designed to track one of their indexes, and, in this case, US real estate companies and REITs.

- DBC (Invesco DB Commodity Index ETF):[29] For broad-based commodity exposure
- DBMF (iMGP DBi Managed Futures Strategy ETF): For exposure to managed futures, offering a potential hedge in market downturns[30]

While some alternatives have higher fees than stocks or bonds, these are relatively low-cost and accessible through major brokerages.

Interpretation

If you are just getting started with investing, it's easy to feel overwhelmed by all the choices. The good news is that you do not need to make things complicated. Many long-term investors begin with a total market stock ETF like VTI or SCHB and a broad bond ETF like BND as a simple foundation. These types of funds are well-diversified, low-cost, and efficient, which means more of your money stays invested and working for you.

Cash and cash equivalents may not seem exciting, but they play a vital role in your overall financial picture. High-yield savings accounts or money market funds like VMFXX provide liquidity and stability, especially for emergency savings or short-term needs. Once that is in place, you might consider adding real estate exposure through REIT ETFs like VNQ or

---

29 In the Invesco DB Commodity Index ETF, DB refers to Deutsche Bank, which created the underlying commodity index the fund tracks.

30 iMGP DBi Managed Futures Strategy ETF is an exchange-traded fund managed by Investment Managers Group Partners (iMGP) and designed by Dynamic Beta investments (DBi) that aims to replicate hedge fund–style managed futures strategies in a liquid and lower-cost ETF format.

SCHH, which offer access to property markets without the hassle of direct ownership. Optional alternatives like gold or commodity ETFs can be layered in over time as part of a diversification strategy.

The key is to keep investing simple, low-cost, and diversified. Understand what you own, set an asset allocation that fits your goals, and automate contributions where possible. Automation builds discipline, keeps emotions in check, and helps you stay on track over time. Do not feel like you have to cover every asset class at once because you can expand gradually as your experience and portfolio grow.

Example Prompt with Output and Interpretation

Prompt

"If someone wanted a diversified portfolio that they could build and hold onto for a long time, what would you recommend and why?"

AI Output

If someone is looking to build a long-term, diversified portfolio that they can mostly set and forget, I'd recommend a three-fund portfolio as a starting point. It's simple, cost-effective, and globally diversified across asset classes. Below is the basic breakdown:

- US Total Stock Market ETF (e.g., VTI or SCHB): It gives you broad exposure to thousands of US companies of all sizes. It's a core growth engine for long-term wealth.

- International Total Stock Market ETF (e.g., VXUS or IXUS): It adds global diversification, including developed and emerging markets, thereby reducing your reliance on US market performance.
- Total Bond Market ETF (e.g., BND or AGG): It provides stability and income, helping smooth out the ride when markets get choppy.[31]

You can adjust the allocation between these three based on your risk tolerance and time horizon. For example, a younger investor with a high-risk tolerance might choose 80% stocks (split between US and international markets) and 20% bonds. A more conservative or older investor might prefer a 60% stocks/40% bonds mix. This approach keeps fees low, avoids unnecessary complexity, and still checks all the boxes: growth, income, and diversification.

If you want to go one step further, you can layer in REITs (e.g., VNQ) for real estate exposure or treasury inflation-protected securities (TIPS)[32] for inflation pro-

---

31 VTI (Vanguard Total Stock Market ETF) and SCHB (Schwab US Broad Market ETF) track the overall US stock market. VXUS (Vanguard Total International Stock ETF) and IXUS (iShares Core MSCI Total International Stock ETF) cover non-US stocks across developed and emerging markets. BND (Vanguard Total Bond Market ETF) and AGG (iShares Core US Aggregate Bond ETF) represent the broad US bond market.

32 Treasury Inflation-Protected Securities are government bonds designed to keep up with inflation, and their value rises when prices rise. They can represent a good way to protect the purchasing power of your money over time, especially during periods of higher inflation.

tection, but the three-fund strategy alone is often more than enough. The most important thing is not timing or tinkering; it's consistency and staying invested over decades.

Interpretation

If you want a long-term, diversified portfolio, you really don't need to overcomplicate it. A simple three-fund setup does the job: US stocks for growth, international stocks for global balance, and bonds for stability. You just adjust the mix based on your age and risk tolerance—more stocks if you're younger and can handle the ups and downs, more bonds if you want a smoother ride. It's low-cost, easy to manage, and gives you everything you need: growth, income, and diversification. Stick with it, stay consistent, and let time do the heavy lifting.

Example Prompt with Output and Interpretation

Prompt

"I am concerned about large US technology firms driving the returns of the US stock market. What would you recommend I do with my portfolio to address this concern?"

AI Output

That's a valid concern. Recent returns in the US stock market have been heavily concentrated in a handful of large-cap tech companies. If you're uncomfortable with that level of concentration risk, below are a few ways to adjust your portfolio to spread out your exposure:

- Tilt Toward Equal-Weight or Multi-Factor ETFs: Instead of market-cap-weighted funds (like VTI or SPY), consider equal-weight ETFs (like RSP) that give every stock the same weight, so you're not overexposed to the biggest companies. You could also look at multi-factor ETFs (like AVUS or VFMF) that emphasize factors like value, quality, or small-cap, which diversify away from pure growth and mega-cap tech.[33]
- Increase Exposure to Small- and Mid-Cap Stocks: Add or overweight a small-cap ETF like VBR (small-cap value) or AVUV, which tends to be less correlated with the performance of large tech.[34]
- Boost International Allocation: International markets tend to be less tech-heavy and more value-oriented, so increasing your allocation to ETFs like VXUS (total international) or VWO (emerging markets) can help balance things out.

---

33 VTI (Vanguard Total Stock Market ETF) and SPY (SPDR S&P 500 ETF) are market-cap-weighted funds where the largest companies drive most of the returns. RSP (Invesco S&P 500 Equal Weight ETF) gives every company the same weight, helping reduce that concentration. AVUS (Avantis US Equity ETF) and VFMF (Vanguard US Multifactor ETF) tilt toward factors like value, quality, and smaller size. Using these types of ETFs can help balance a portfolio that's become too dependent on large cap growth stocks.

34 VBR (Vanguard Small Cap Value ETF) and AVUV (Avantis US Small Cap Value ETF) focus on smaller, value-oriented companies that often behave differently from large cap growth stocks. Therefore, increasing exposure to these areas can help reduce portfolio concentration and add diversification.

- Add Sector Diversification: You could also add exposure to underrepresented sectors like industrials, energy, or healthcare using sector ETFs if you want to make more targeted tilts.[35]

If you're uneasy about the dominance of US tech giants, the solution is to lean more into small-cap, value, international, or equal-weight strategies, all of which can reduce reliance on the "Magnificent Seven"[36] without abandoning long-term growth potential.

Interpretation

It is completely valid to be concerned about the extent to which large US technology companies have been driving market returns recently. A handful of mega-cap names have dominated performance, and while that is not unusual in certain cycles, it can make your portfolio feel overly dependent on just a few companies. That said, this kind of concentration has happened before and is not necessarily a reason to panic or abandon US stocks altogether.

---

35 VTI (Vanguard Total Stock Market), SPY (SPDR S&P 500), RSP (Invesco S&P 500 Equal Weight), AVUS (Avantis US Equity), VFMF (Vanguard US Multifactor), VBR (Vanguard Small-Cap Value), AVUV (Avantis US Small-Cap Value), VXUS (Vanguard Total International Stock), and VWO (Vanguard FTSE Emerging Markets) are all ETFs that track different slices of the stock market.

36 The "Magnificent Seven" refers to a group of large US technology and growth companies (Apple, Microsoft, Amazon, Alphabet, Meta, Nvidia, and Tesla) that have driven a significant share of recent stock market gains.

If it is something that bothers you, there are ways to gently rebalance without overhauling your whole portfolio. You can add equal-weight ETFs so every stock carries the same weight, tilt more toward small-cap or value stocks, or increase your international exposure since those markets tend to be less tech-heavy. These small shifts can reduce your reliance on just a few names while keeping you broadly invested and set up for long-term growth.

Additional Ways to Use AI for Investment Ideas

If you upload the list of funds available in your workplace retirement plan, such as a 401(k), 403(b), or TSP, along with your preferred asset allocation and risk profile, AI can help you sort through the noise and figure out exactly what to pick. Most plans offer a mix of stock funds, bond funds, and, sometimes, target-date or stable value funds; however, the quality of those options can vary. AI can go through your list and apply the same criteria previously mentioned (e.g., low costs and broad diversification) to the recommended funds based on your goals.

Investing Sample Prompts

Broad Market
- "List five US total market ETFs with expense ratios under 0.05%, sorted by five-year annualized returns."

- "Compare VTI, SCHB, and ITOT based on expense ratio, average daily volume, and tracking error versus the CRSP US Total Market Index."[37]

Value Versus Growth

- "What are the top ETFs for US large-cap value exposure with at least $5 billion in AUM and a dividend yield over 2%?"
- "Compare SPYG and VUG on historical performance, sector weightings, and valuation metrics."[38]

Small and Mid Cap

- "Find three US small-cap ETFs with low expense ratios and exposure to the Russell 2000 Index.[39] Which has the lowest tracking error?"
- "Compare IJR, VB, and SCHA on risk-adjusted return over the past 10 years."[40]

---

37 CRSP stands for the Center for Research in Security Prices, which develops widely used stock market indexes. The CRSP US Total Market Index tracks nearly all publicly traded U.S. companies across large-, mid-, small-cap stocks.

38 SPYG (SPDR Portfolio S&P 500 Growth ETF, tracks growth stocks within the S&P 500) and VUG (Vanguard Growth ETF, tracks US large-cap growth stocks).

39 The Russell 2000 Index tracks about 2,000 of the smallest publicly traded US companies, making it a common benchmark for small-cap stock performance.

40 IJR (iShares Core S&P Small-Cap ETF, tracks US small-cap stocks), VB (Vanguard Small-Cap ETF, broad small-cap exposure), SCHA (Schwab US Small-Cap ETF, tracks the Dow Jones US Small-Cap Index).

International Stocks (Developed Markets and Emerging Markets)

- "What are the best ETFs for developed markets (excluding the US)? Compare them based on cost and country breakdown."
- "Compare the top mutual funds that invest in large-cap companies outside the US, highlighting performance, fees, and any key differences."
- "Find ETFs that track emerging markets with exposure to Asia, Africa, and Latin America. Focus on funds with over $1 billion AUM and low turnover."

Bonds

- "List five intermediate-term bond mutual funds with low fees and a track record of outperforming their category over the last five years."
- "What are the best ETFs for US Treasury exposure across short, intermediate, and long durations?"
- "Find funds focused solely on TIPS and compare their yield and duration."
- "List investment-grade corporate bond ETFs with low expense ratios and at least a 3% yield. Compare credit quality and sector allocation."

Cash and Cash Equivalents

- "List money market mutual funds with yields above 4% and zero transaction fees."
- "Compare ultra-short bond ETFs like JPST, ICSH, and MINT for stability, yield, and interest rate sensitivity."[41]

---

41 JPST (J. P. Morgan Ultra-Short Income ETF), ICSH (iShares Ultra Short-Term Bond ETF), and MINT (PIMCO Enhanced Short Maturity

Multi-Asset/Target-Date/Balanced Funds[42]

- "Find balanced mutual funds with a 60% stocks/40% bonds allocation, low fees, and a strong long-term track record."
- "Compare target-date funds for someone retiring in 2045, specifically from Vanguard, Fidelity, and T. Rowe Price, based on glide path[43], equity exposure, and fees."

Tax Efficiency and Fund Structure

- "Which US stock ETFs have the best tax efficiency over the past five years based on turnover, distribution history, and structure?"
- "Compare mutual funds versus ETFs in the same category for tax efficiency. Use VTSAX and VTI as examples."

Strategy-Based Prompts

- "I want to build a globally diversified portfolio with a 70% stocks/30% bonds mix. Which funds would you recommend for each component if I want to keep fees below 0.10%?"

Active ETF) are ultra-short bond funds designed to offer modest yield and low volatility with limited interest rate risk.

42 Multi-asset, target-date, and balanced funds are all types of investments that combine multiple asset classes—typically, stocks, bonds, and (sometimes) cash—into a single fund for diversification. Balanced funds usually maintain a fixed mix (like 60% stocks, 40% bonds), while target-date funds automatically shift from aggressive to conservative as you approach a specific retirement year. These funds are designed to simplify investing by providing a diversified, all-in-one solution based on your risk level and/or time horizon.

43 A glide path is the formula that gradually shifts a portfolio' s mix of stocks and bonds over time, usually reducing risk as you approach retirement.

- "Build a portfolio of five ETFs for a long-term investor with moderate risk tolerance, global diversification, and a tilt toward value and dividends."

You will want to inform your AI tool how aggressive or conservative you wish to be, and it will help you break that allocation down into the best available funds in each category. For example, if you are looking for growth and can handle some volatility, it will lean toward equity funds. Alternatively, if you are more risk-averse or closer to retirement, it will incorporate more fixed income or stability. This can save you considerable time and frustration, especially if your plan includes a long list of confusing or redundant options. Moreover, this approach can help you take control of your investing strategy without making it your full-time job.

CHAPTER 9

WHAT ABOUT ALTERNATIVES?

"In alternative investing, the return of your capital
is just as important as the return on your capital."
—*Unknown*

Alternative investments can be defined as anything outside traditional stocks, bonds, and cash. These can include private equity, hedge funds, real estate, commodities, venture capital, private credit, collectibles like art or wine, and even cryptocurrencies. Historically, they have been utilized by institutions and high-net-worth investors. However, access has expanded in recent years. Many 401(k) plans still exclude them, but accredited investors often gain access through private funds, platforms, or self-directed IRAs.

These investments tend to be less liquid, less regulated, and more opaque than traditional investments. While this is not necessarily a negative, it means investors need to conduct more due diligence. For those with a long-time horizon, high risk tolerance, and the ability to handle illiquidity, alternatives can offer powerful diversification. Their returns may not move in sync with the stock market, which can help smoothen volatility. However, they may also carry unique risks such as manager risk,[44] leverage, valuation uncertainty, and lack of daily pricing, to name a few.

Who Can Invest in Alternatives?

A factor people often overlook when considering alternative investments is whether they are even eligible to access certain options. In some cases, you must qualify as what the Securities and Exchange Commission (SEC) refers to as an accredited investor. This designation applies to individuals who meet specific income, net worth, or professional requirements. Generally, this means earning more than $200,000 annually as an individual (or $300,000 with a spouse) for each of the previous two years, with the expectation of the same in the present year, or having a net worth of more than $1 million, excluding your primary residence.

There are also alternative pathways to accreditation for those who hold certain professional licenses, such as the Series 65, Series 7, or Series 82, which broaden the definition beyond just wealth. The purpose of the accredited investor rule is to limit access to more complex and less regulated private investments to individuals who are presumed to have the financial

---

44 Manager risk refers to the possibility that an actively managed fund underperforms not because of market conditions but because of the fund manager's decisions. Even skilled managers can make poor calls, such as choosing the wrong securities, mistiming trades, or drifting from their stated strategy.

sophistication and risk tolerance to evaluate them appropriately. The assumption is that accredited investors can afford the risk and handle potential losses.

Do you need to be an accredited investor to invest in alternatives? Well, it depends. Some alternative investments, such as hedge funds, private equity, venture capital, and private credit funds, are restricted to accredited investors only. This is because these types of alternative investments do not go through the same disclosure and regulatory processes as publicly traded investments. However, not all alternatives are gated. Publicly traded REITs and commodities ETFs are some examples of alternative investments available to anyone.

AI can provide valuable assistance in navigating the alternative investment space, as it can help screen private deals, summarize offering memoranda, and even evaluate sentiment trends for cryptocurrencies. Furthermore, with the right inputs, AI can assist in comparing fund structures, calculating internal rates of return, and pointing out red flags in pitch decks. While alternatives still require judgment and due diligence, AI can significantly reduce the time spent gathering and processing information.

Here are example prompts with AI output to show how it can support this process:

Example Prompt with Output and Interpretation

Prompt

"Do you recommend investing in cryptocurrencies, and if so, what is the safest and best way to invest in them?"

AI Output

Although I do not recommend crypto as a core part of your portfolio, it can make sense as a small satellite position if you (a) understand the risks, (b) can handle high volatility, and (c) are investing with money you can afford to lose.

Cryptocurrencies are speculative; they do not produce cash flows like stocks or interest like bonds, so their value is driven primarily by supply, demand, and sentiment. This makes it risky and difficult to value.

If you decide to invest in cryptocurrencies, the following is the safest way:

- Keep your allocation small (typically no more than 1–5% of your total portfolio).
- Stick to the most established cryptocurrencies, such as Bitcoin (BTC) or Ethereum (ETH). These are the most widely used and have the most developed infrastructure.
- Use a reputable platform for buying and holding:
  - For beginners: Use Coinbase, Fidelity Crypto, or Robinhood (which offer a simple user interface and regulatory oversight).
  - For more control: Use a hardware wallet (like Ledger) to store cryptocurrencies offline after purchasing.
- Consider cryptocurrency ETFs if you prefer not to hold cryptocurrencies directly. These allow you to gain exposure without dealing with wallets or exchanges. For example:
  - BITO: A Bitcoin futures ETF

o   IBIT or FBTC: spot Bitcoin ETFs (if available through your broker)[45]

In summary, treat crypto like venture capital. Use funds or platforms with strong security and regulatory oversight, and ensure the rest of your portfolio is stable, diversified, and built to last.

Interpretation

Cryptocurrencies can play a role in a portfolio, but they should be treated as a speculative side bet rather than a core holding. They are high-risk and highly volatile, and unlike stocks or bonds, they do not produce income or cash flow, which makes their value largely dependent on sentiment and speculation. If you decide to invest, keep it simple by sticking with established options and using reputable platforms like Coinbase, Fidelity, or even a spot Bitcoin ETF to avoid the hassle of wallets. A small allocation can give you exposure to an emerging space, but the foundation of your portfolio should remain grounded in proven, long-term strategies.

---

45   BITO (ProShares Bitcoin Strategy ETF) gives exposure to Bitcoin through future contracts rather than holding the asset directly. IBIT (iShares Bitcoin Trust) and FBTC (Fidelity Wise Origin Bitcoin Fund) are spot Bitcoin ETFs that hold actual Bitcoin. These funds make it easier to gain crypto exposure in a traditional brokerage account without managing digital wallets.

Example Prompt with Output and Interpretation

Prompt

"List the top US private credit ETFs available, along with their investment strategies and fees."

AI Output

Below are the top US-listed private credit ETFs, along with their investment strategies and fee structures, for investors looking to access private credit exposure in a liquid ETF:

SPDR State Street Global Advisors (SSGA) Apollo IG Public and Private Credit ETF (PRIV)
- Strategy: It is an actively managed hybrid fund blending investment-grade public credit with 10–35% private credit exposure sourced and backed by Apollo Global Management. The remainder of the portfolio remains in liquid, public instruments.
- Expense Ratio: 0.70%
- Why it matters: This fund offers retail investors one of the first ETF vehicles to exceed the typical 15% illiquid holdings limit by leveraging Apollo's liquidity facility. This structure introduces complexity and liquidity risks under stress.

BondBloxx Private Credit CLO ETF (PCMM)
- Strategy: It is actively managed and invests at least 80% of net assets in collateralized loan obligations (CLOs) backed by middle-market private

corporate loans. The fund seeks capital preservation and current income.[46]

- Expense Ratio: 0.68%
- Yield: Target yield is typically in the 7–8%+ range.

Virtus Private Credit Strategy ETF (VPC)

- Strategy: It passively tracks the Indxx Private Credit Index, which includes US-listed closed-end funds (many business development companies (BDCs) and specialty finance funds) with a focus on private credit strategies. This fund offers index-based exposure to public vehicles investing in private credit.
- Expense Ratio: Approximately 0.75% (primarily due to underlying fund expense layers; the ETF structure fee itself is minimal)
- Yield: Dividend yield is often around 11–12%, though total return and fees net of yield can vary significantly.

Key Considerations

- Higher Fees: All three ETFs charge significantly more in fees than typical public bond ETFs (which often cost ≤ 0.10%). The elevated costs reflect access to complex, often illiquid credit strategies.
- Liquidity Risk: Some private credit exposure relies on contractual liquidity commitments (especially

---

46　This fund is actively managed and focuses on CLOs, which are bundles of corporate loans packaged together and sold to investors. Most of these loans come from private, mid-sized companies. The goal is to preserve capital while generating steady income, though the loans carry more credit risk than government or investment-grade bonds.

PRIV). Market stress might impair smooth re-demption or pricing. The SEC has highlighted these concerns as part of recent approvals.

- Complex Underlying Structures: VPC invests via publicly listed closed-end funds, which may include leverage and discount/premium risks. CLO-based strategies like PCMM also have struc-tural complexity. These are not your average bond holdings.

If you are considering adding private credit via ETF exposure, these three are the primary options in the US market today. They offer a mix of exposure types, from hybrid models with liquidity buffers (PRIV) to concentrated CLO structures (PCMM) and broader index-like access via listed credit vehicles (VPC), each of which comes with different fee structures, structural risks, and yield expectations.

Interpretation

Private credit ETFs offer a new way for everyday in-vestors to access a corner of the market that was previ-ously reserved for institutions and accredited investors. These funds provide exposure to private loans, often issued to middle-market companies, and can offer attractive yields relative to traditional fixed income. While the income potential is appealing, private cred-it ETFs are not necessarily suitable for every investor. Moreover, they often carry higher fees, and their un-derlying assets may be illiquid or difficult to price in volatile markets. Unlike traditional bond ETFs, which hold highly liquid treasuries and/or investment-grade corporates, private credit ETFs can rely on complex credit instruments and facilities to provide daily liquidity. This can result in additional risk, especially in a credit event or market stress, where pricing or redemptions might not behave as expected. Further, they are also more sensitive to credit quality deterioration and may not provide the same level of downside protection as investment-grade bonds.

For investors with a high-risk tolerance looking to diversify their income sources beyond public markets, a small allocation to private credit ETFs may seem sensible. However, they should be viewed as a complement, not a replacement, for core bond holdings. Therefore, as with any alternative investment, it is critical to understand the structure, fees, and liquidity profile before proceeding. These ETFs make private credit more accessible, but that accessibility does not eliminate the risks that have gone away.

Example Prompt with Output and Interpretation

Prompt

"Evaluate this potential commercial real estate investment for an individual investor. List the good, the bad, and the ugly. Assume I will need a loan from a bank to purchase this, and consider the current lending environment in your response. (Upload the property offering memorandum or marketing flyer with the prompt.)"

AI Output[47]

Based on the offering flyer for 123 Anywhere Lane, Small Town, US, here's a detailed evaluation of the commercial real estate investment opportunity, assuming you are financing it with a bank loan in the current (mid-2025) lending environment.

The Good

1. Strong Lease Profile
   o The property is fully leased to ABC Inc. through August 31, 2030, providing over five years of lease term remaining.
   o The lease includes 3% annual rent escalations, which is above average in the current market and will help offset inflation and future interest rate increases.
   o It's a triple net (NNN) lease, meaning that the tenant is responsible for taxes, insurance, and maintenance, thus reducing your operating responsibilities and protecting your net operating income (NOI).
2. Income-Producing with Reasonable Cap Rate
   o Purchase price: $2,500,000
   o NOI (as of 9/1/2025): $174,000
   o This implies a 6.96% cap rate, which is attractive in today's market, especially for a property with a strong lease and no landlord responsibilities.

---

47 The original output is included here, though the property address has been redacted for confidentiality.

3. Functional Industrial Asset
   o The building is 15,555 square feet on two acres, split between office and warehouse space.
   o Features include the following:
     • Multiple drive-in doors
     • Standing seam metal roof
     • Geothermal heating, ventilation, and air conditioning (HVAC) and solar panels (potential for energy efficiency and reduced tenant operating costs)
   o Zoning: Industrial
   o The asset is modern, flexible, and functional, appealing to both the current tenant and future users.

The Bad

1. Tenant Credit Unknown
   o ABC Inc. may be a regional or local HVAC/plumbing company. No credit rating or financials are provided in the flyer, so you will need to assess their balance sheet, profitability, and debt load to understand default risk.
   o While trades-based businesses can be stable, their creditworthiness can vary greatly.
2. Market Depth & Exit Liquidity
   o The asset is located in Small Town, US, which is a coastal town and not a core industrial market like Raleigh, Charlotte, or Wilmington.
   o This limits your buyer pool at exit and may create valuation pressure if cap rates expand or the lease term is short when you go to sell.

o Lenders may apply a haircut to values or underwrite more conservatively in secondary or tertiary markets.

3. Potential Financing Headwinds
   o Given the current lending environment:
     • Most banks are offering 60% to 65% loan-to-value (LTV).
     • Interest rates are likely between 7% and 8% for investor-owned NNN deals in secondary markets.
     • If the tenant lacks audited financials or a personal/corporate guarantee, that may further constrain loan terms.
   o You will likely need $875,000 to $1 million in equity, and the debt service coverage ratio (DSCR) will need to be modeled carefully, given rate pressure.

The Ugly

1. Single-Tenant Risk
   o All your income depends on one tenant, in one building, in one location.
   o If ABC Inc. leaves in 2030—or worse, defaults earlier—you could be left with a vacant building, little income, and ongoing debt service obligations.
   o Re-leasing in Small Town, US, could take time and may require tenant improvement (TI) allowances or concessions.

2. No Co-Tenant or Expansion Buffer
   o There is no indication of additional tenant space or expansion opportunity on the lot.

This limits the flexibility if the current tenant downsizes or if you need to repurpose the space.

3. Limited Visibility into Lease Terms
    o   The flyer lacks details on any guarantees or security deposits and information on who pays utilities, capital expenses, or major repairs (claimed NNN, but needs verification).

Quick Financial Snapshot (Assumed Financing)
- Purchase Price: $2,500,000
- NOI: $174,000
- Assumed Loan: 65% LTV = $1,625,000
- Interest Rate: 7.5%, 20-year amortization
- Annual Debt Service: Approximately $153,100
- Cash Flow Before Taxes: Approximately $20,900
- Cash-on-Cash Return: Approximately 2.4% (on $875,000 equity)

This means that nearly all of your returns in the early years come from rent growth and future appreciation, not cash flow. You would need to confirm the actual rent and lender terms to refine this further.

Bottom Line
This is a clean, stabilized NNN deal in a coastal secondary market with a solid cap rate and a long lease— all good ingredients. However, you will need to carefully assess the tenant's credit, lease specifics, and your financing terms to determine if the thin cash flow is acceptable relative to the risk.

Recommended next steps are as follows:
- Request the full lease agreement.
- Review tenant financials or any credit history.
- Confirm lender appetite for the deal and prequalify financing.
- Run a sensitivity analysis on vacancy risk and exit cap rates.

If you are looking for a steady income with a hands-off structure and can accept modest cash flow with more back-end upside, this could be a reasonable pick. However, if you want yield or appreciation through value-add, this likely isn't the right choice.

Interpretation

This property offers a stable, long-term lease with 3% annual rent increases, backed by a local HVAC and plumbing tenant through 2030. It is a true triple net lease, which means minimal landlord responsibilities, and the nearly 7% cap rate is attractive in today's market. Further, the building is well-equipped and is priced at a level that is accessible to some individual investors. For someone looking for mailbox money, this checks several boxes.

There are a few aspects to watch closely. The tenant's credit quality is not disclosed, and the market, while growing, is still a secondary market, which limits your exit strategy options. With rising interest rates and conservative bank underwriting, you would likely need to bring around 35–40% equity to the table, and even then, cash flow could be thin. As with any single-tenant deal, vacancy risk is concentrated, and if the tenant leaves, you are responsible until you can re-lease or sell. Therefore, you need to confirm the lease terms, rent escalations, and tenant financials before proceeding further.

With the right inputs, AI can quickly summarize potential properties, highlight the strengths and weak-nesses of potential deals, identify missing data, mod-el cash flows under various loan terms, and compare similar properties or cap rates in the area. You can also ask it to break down debt service coverage ratios, eval-uate sensitivity to interest rate changes, or even assess tenant concentration risk in your portfolio. AI cannot replace the final decision that you will ultimately make, but it can reduce the time spent gathering and organiz-ing information so that you can focus on making sound investment decisions.

Alternative Investments Sample Prompts

Real Estate and Private Equity

- "Find US-focused REIT ETFs with at least $500 million in AUM, low expense ratios, and exposure to commercial real estate."
- "Compare leading real estate ETFs by dividend yield, sec-tor allocation, and performance during rising rate environ-ments. Highlight differences among the most commonly used funds."
- "Which international REIT mutual funds have historically outperformed in low-interest-rate periods?"

- "Summarize the key risks and return drivers of this private real estate offering memorandum."
- "What is the cap rate trend in industrial properties in Florida over the past five years?"
- "Compare the Internal Rate of Return (IRR), equity multiple, and fee structure of these private equity fund term sheets (upload term sheets)."

Commodities

- "What are the top commodity ETFs with diversified exposure to energy, metals, and agriculture? Compare expense ratios and tracking methods."
- "Compare popular gold ETFs in terms of long-term performance, fees, and overall suitability for investors. Which option stands out as the better choice net of costs?"

Hedge Funds and Structured Products

- "Explain the strategy and downside risk of this long/short hedge fund based on its summary (upload details of the fund)."
- "Which hedge fund strategies are least correlated with the S&P 500?"
- "Analyze this structured note's payoff structure and break down its risk-return profile in simple terms."

General Due Diligence

- "Create a checklist of questions to ask before investing in a private credit fund."
- "Summarize the pros and cons of investing in collectibles like fine art or vintage wine."
- "Identify red flags in this alternative investment pitch deck."

Alternatives: Optional, Not Essential

Alternative investments such as private equity, hedge funds, real estate, private credit, and cryptocurrencies can offer diversification and, in some cases, higher returns. They also come with added complexity, limited liquidity, and less transparency than traditional stocks and bonds. You do not need them to build wealth or reach your goals. For most investors, a portfolio of low-cost, broadly diversified index funds combined with consistent saving and investing is more than enough. If alternatives feel overwhelming or do not align with your philosophy, there is absolutely no pressure to include them.

If you are interested in exploring alternatives, AI can make the process more approachable. It can summarize offering materials, compare fund structures, model potential returns, and highlight unusual terms, saving time and providing a clearer view of a space that is often opaque. Still, AI has its limits. It cannot verify the accuracy of numbers in a private deal, assess the true quality of a fund manager, or interpret the fine print in complex legal documents. It is a helpful research assistant, not a fiduciary.

Ultimately, alternatives may suit investors who understand the risks and want to diversify income or reduce exposure to traditional markets. For many others, skipping them is the better choice. The best portfolio is not the most complicated; it is the one you understand, believe in, and can stay committed to through all market conditions.

CHAPTER 10

TEST BEFORE YOU INVEST

"Forecasts may tell you a great deal about the forecaster;
they tell you nothing about the future."
—Warren Buffett

One of the most common questions I hear from people when they start thinking about investing is: "How do I know if I am making the right decision?" It is a fair question. Nobody wants to invest money only to watch it lose value, after all. While no one can predict the future perfectly, one of the most powerful things you can do is test your strategy before you commit real dollars. That is where AI can help significantly.

This chapter focuses on how you can use AI to backtest past performance, forecast possible future outcomes, and simulate how your investing decisions might play out. You do not need to be a math whiz or a Wall Street veteran to use these tools. What you do need is curiosity, a desire to learn, and a willingness to think through the "what ifs" of investing.

What Is Backtesting, and Why Does It Matter?

Backtesting is a simple but powerful concept that involves taking a strategy or investment idea and testing it using past data to see how it would have performed. Imagine saying, "If I had invested in these five ETFs five years ago and rebalanced once a year, how would I have done?" That is a backtest. AI can help you automate this process. You can upload or link data, run comparisons, calculate returns, and even account for factors like fees and taxes. It provides a way to learn from history before risking your own money.

Investing is not about guarantees but rather about probabilities. Backtesting helps you understand the likelihood that a strategy might work again. It will not tell you the future, but it can highlight strengths, weaknesses, and patterns worth noting. Let's say you are considering allocating your portfolio 60% in US stocks, 30% in international stocks, and 10% in bonds. Backtesting allows you to ask: How would that mix have performed over the last 10, 20, or even 30 years? What would the ups and downs have looked like? Would it have helped or hurt during recessions? That kind of insight can help you build something that feels good on paper and even better in practice.

However, a word of caution about backtests is in order. They cannot predict the future; what they do is operate on the assumption that the past can offer a reasonable guide, which is not a guarantee. Forecasts are only as good as the data and models you provide, and you must be wary of common traps that can make results appear better than they really are.[48] These pitfalls, such as survivorship bias, look-ahead bias, and

---

48 When backtesting, a data checklist prompt like this can be helpful: List the data sources, assumptions, and biases that could affect this backtest. Show me how each might change the results.

overfitting, can quietly creep into your analysis and distort your conclusions. Survivorship bias happens when the data only include investments that still exist today, leaving out those that failed and disappeared. Look-ahead bias happens when your test inadvertently uses information that would not have been available at the time, which can give an unfair advantage. Overfitting occurs when a strategy is tailored so perfectly to past data that it performs beautifully in history but falls apart in the real world. Thus, understanding and avoiding these biases can help you run tests that provide a clearer and more realistic picture of how your strategy might hold up.

Thinking Ahead with Better Data

Forecasting is the art and science of looking forward. You take what you know—historical data, market trends, interest rates, inflation, company earnings, and global risks—and try to estimate what might happen next. It is not magic, but when you combine solid data with good modeling, it can help you think about the future.

AI excels in this area because it can process massive amounts of information at once. Whether it is analyzing inflation trends, bond yield curves, earnings reports, or global events, AI can synthesize the data quickly and offer a range of likely outcomes. It does not necessarily provide one answer, but it helps you understand possible paths the market might take.

When you use ChatGPT or another AI model to forecast, you can use a question such as the following:

- "What might a 60% stocks/40% bonds portfolio return in the next 10 years based on historical returns and current market conditions?"

- "If interest rates rise by 1%, how could that affect the performance of long-term bond funds?"
- "What sectors have historically performed well after a recession?"

AI uses historical context and models to offer educated scenarios. The goal is not to achieve perfection but to make better decisions by thinking ahead.

What If Your Plan Meets Real Life?

Simulation is where things become particularly interesting. This is where you ask, "If I do X and the market does Y, what will happen?" It allows you to test different inputs and assumptions to see how your financial plan holds up. Let's say you want to retire in 20 years. You invest $1,000 per month and invest in a diversified portfolio. What would your portfolio look like if you achieve 7% returns? What if it is only 4%? What if there is a bear market five years before retirement? Simulations help answer those questions.[49]

AI can run these scenarios rather quickly. You provide your income, your savings rate, and target retirement age, and it can simulate a path for you. Then, you adjust the numbers and see what changes. One popular simulation approach is called Monte Carlo, which runs your plan thousands of times with different assumptions each time. The output is a probability of success. For example, you might see, "You have a 78% chance of reaching your goal if market returns are average and you continue saving as planned."

---

49 Tools like PortfolioVisualizer.com can be great for this.

However, please be mindful of the behavioral aspects of simulations. Even the most impressive simulation on paper can falter if you abandon the plan when markets become turbulent. This is where the behavioral side of investing comes into play. Simulations assume you will follow the strategy exactly as modeled, even if circumstances change. When markets drop sharply, fear and loss aversion can push investors to sell at the worst possible time or to pause investing altogether just when future returns are most attractive. Conversely, when markets rise, overconfidence and greed can tempt investors to take on more risk. Therefore, remember that a simulation is only as good as your ability to adhere to the plan that you are testing.

Test Before You Invest Sample Prompts

Before committing to any investment strategy, it helps to see how it might have performed in the past or under different conditions. Here are a few example prompts:

- Ask About Historical Returns: "What was the average annual return of the S&P 500 over the last 20 years, including dividends?"
- Compare Different Strategies: "If I invested $10,000 in VTI (US total market ETF) versus QQQ (Nasdaq 100 ETF) starting in 2010 and held until today, what would the total return and ending balance be for each?"[50]

---

50 VTI is the Vanguard Total Stock Market ETF, covering nearly the entire US equity market. QQQ is the Invesco ETF that tracks the Nasdaq 100 Index, which is heavily weighted toward large technology and growth companies.

- Incorporate Rebalancing: "Backtest a 60% stocks/40% bonds portfolio rebalanced annually from 2000 to 2023. Assume the 60% was in VTI and 40% in BND."[51]
- Include Withdrawals or Contributions: "Simulate a $500 monthly investment from January 2010 to December 2024 into a three-fund portfolio: 50% VTI (US stocks), 30% VXUS (international stocks), and 20% BND (bonds). Include total contributions, ending balance, and annualized return."[52]

One of the biggest advantages of using AI in your investing process is not necessarily obtaining the perfect answer; rather, it is gaining a richer picture of the possibilities. Forecasting and simulation are two areas where AI can truly excel, especially when you are trying to make long-term decisions in a constantly changing world. It will not provide tomorrow's stock prices or guarantee what your portfolio will be worth in 30 years, but it can give you the next best thing: context, historical perspective, and a way to model "what if" scenarios so that you can make better-informed decisions.

Below are some additional example prompts:
- "Given current inflation and interest rate trends, what might bond returns look like over the next 5 years?" *This helps you think about how rising or falling rates impact bond prices and yields. AI can walk you through historical parallels (like the 1970s or post-2008 period) and help you weigh the trade-offs between short- and long-duration bonds.*

---

51 BND is the Vanguard Total Bond Market ETF, giving broad exposure to US investment-grade bonds.
52 VXUS is the Vanguard Total International Stock ETF, which holds thousands of companies outside the US, including both developed and emerging markets.

- "How do high CAPE ratios[53] affect future stock market returns historically?"

  The CAPE ratio is one of those metrics that tends to predict long-run stock returns reasonably well, especially over 10–15 year periods. Ask AI to summarize past outcomes when the CAPE was high, and it will help you think about what might come next.

- "Compare the outlook for US stocks and international stocks over the next decade."

  You will not get a precise forecast, but you will get a thoughtful answer about valuation differences, economic growth forecasts, currency risks, and diversification benefits. It can also help you consider what scenarios might favor one region over another.

- "If a recession hits in the next year, how have defensive stocks historically performed?"

  You could see how sectors such as utilities, healthcare, and consumer staples have behaved in past downturns and how they have helped reduce volatility or preserve capital.

- "What happens to dividend-paying stocks when interest rates rise?"

  This prompt encourages an analysis of how rising interest rates might make dividend stocks appear less attractive (relative to bonds) and which types of dividend-paying companies tend to weather rate hikes better than others.

These types of prompts are not just about getting answers; they also help you learn and build your mental model of the

---

53 The Cyclically Adjusted Price-to-Earnings (CAPE) ratio, also called the Shiller P/E, is named after economist Robert Shiller, who popularized it. It is calculated by taking the current price of a broad stock index, such as the S&P 500, and dividing it by the average of inflation-adjusted earnings from the past ten years. This helps smooth out temporary spikes or drops in profits, giving a clearer sense of whether the market looks historically expensive or inexpensive.

investing world. The more you ask, the more you sharpen your ability to connect the dots. Over time, you move past reacting to headlines and start thinking like an analyst or portfolio manager, steadily improving your investing knowledge and judgment.

Real-Life Simulation Prompts

Forecasting is about what might happen out there, whereas simulation is about what that means for you. This is where planning meets imagination, and AI can help you run the tape forward. When people think about simulation, they often envision sophisticated software running thousands of Monte Carlo trials. Yes, tools like Portfolio Visualizer or professional planning platforms can do that. However, AI can still be incredibly helpful, especially if you are in the early or middle stages of your financial planning journey.

Start with straightforward scenarios, such as the following:
- "If I invest $1,000 per month in a 70% stocks/30% bonds portfolio for 25 years, what might my portfolio be worth assuming 6% average returns?"
  AI can walk through the compound interest math and provide a range of outcomes, including how different return assumptions (say, 5% or 7%) would change your results.
- "How would my plan change if I delayed retirement from 60 years old to 65?"
  You will get a breakdown of how those extra five years could benefit your plan with more time to save, fewer years to fund in retirement, and potentially higher benefits.
- "If inflation averages 4% instead of 2%, how much more do I need to save for retirement?"

AI can walk through the erosion of purchasing power and help you understand how much more you would need to accumulate to maintain the same standard of living.

Now, here is where things get more advanced:

- "Simulate 1,000 Monte Carlo scenarios for my retirement plan. Assume I save $15,000 per year until I am 65 years old, invest with an 80% stocks/20% bonds allocation, and plan to withdraw $60,000 per year in retirement starting at age 65. What is the probability of success, and how does the outcome vary based on different market conditions?"
  AI can simulate scenarios using custom assumptions and models, as well as help you build the framework, along with things like withdrawal strategies.

- "Help me model a worst-case scenario where I retire into a bear market. How do I protect my portfolio from a sequence of returns risk?"
  AI can explain the concept clearly, suggest guardrails (like a cash bucket strategy or dynamic withdrawals), and walk you through example calculations.[54]

You can even go lifestyle-specific:

- "I want to take a mini-retirement in my 40s for two years. How much would I need to save ahead of time, and what happens to my long-term retirement plan?"

---

54 This refers to flexible retirement spending approaches such as a cash bucket strategy where you keep a few years of withdrawals in cash or short-term bonds to ride out market downturns. Dynamic withdrawal rules adjust your spending up or down each year depending on portfolio performance. These strategies are designed to reduce the risk from sequence of returns which is the danger that poor market results early in retirement drain your portfolio faster than expected, even if long term averages look fine.

- "If I buy a $500,000 home in five years with 20% down, how does that affect my investment plan and ability to retire at age 60?"

These types of simulations are where AI truly excels—not by performing all the math (though it can help), but by helping you think through the trade-offs. That is what smart investing is all about: balancing risk and return and weighing the tradeoffs between spending today and saving for tomorrow.

Real-Life Example: Testing Your Portfolio

Let's say you are 35 years old, want to retire in 30 years, and currently have $50,000 saved. You plan to invest $1,000 per month. Below are some steps on how you might use AI to test and simulate your strategy:

Step 1: Ask for Asset Allocation Advice
"Based on a 30-year time horizon and a high risk tolerance, what would be a reasonable stock/bond mix?"

Step 2: Backtest It
"Backtest a 90% stocks/10% bonds portfolio from 2000 to 2024. Show annual return, worst year, and maximum drawdown."

Step 3: Simulate Growth
"If I invest $1,000 per month in this asset allocation mix, what might my balance be in 30 years at 6%, 7%, and 8% annual returns?"

Step 4: Run a Retirement Plan

"Assume I want $70,000 per year for annual spending in retirement. How much would I need to retire at age 65 and sustain that income for 30 years?"

Step 5: Stress Test It

"What if market returns are lower in the first 10 years? How would that impact my retirement plan?"

In about 30 minutes, you have built a basic financial model with different scenarios, and you did it without creating complex spreadsheets.

Being Roughly Right Rather Than Precisely Wrong

In investing, context matters more than precision. You do not need to know whether the S&P 500 will return 8.7% or 9.5% per year over the next decade. What matters is understanding that outcomes depend on factors like valuations, earnings growth, inflation, and interest rates—and what those possibilities mean for your plan.

The beauty of AI is that it makes strategic thinking accessible to everyone. You just need curiosity, a few good prompts, and a willingness to explore—that's all. As John Maynard Keynes once said, "It is better to be roughly right than precisely wrong." That wisdom applies perfectly to investing, as good judgment and reasonable estimates are far more valuable than false precision. The biggest drivers of long-term success are not perfect forecasts or complex spreadsheets, but habits such as saving more, investing consistently, and spending less than you earn. You do not need a crystal ball to achieve your goals; you need discipline, time, and patience for compounding to work its magic.

That said, the following are examples of certain limitations of AI:
- It relies on historical data and assumptions.
- It does not replace personal advice or licensed financial guidance.
- It cannot account for your emotions, behavior, or unexpected life events.
- It may miss tax or legal nuances depending on where you live.

Still, you no longer have to guess with your money or be a spreadsheet expert to test ideas. With AI, you can now backtest strategies, model future outcomes, and simulate your financial plan before committing real dollars. Using AI will not eliminate risk, but it will help you make more informed decisions. If you run an analysis in ChatGPT, try it again in another AI platform. Comparing results can expose differences in assumptions, reveal potential bias, and help you catch errors. Besides, when you see example prompts that ask for current data, such as returns, prices, or valuations, remember that AI may be relying on past information unless it is connected to a live data source or plugin. Without that connection, its answers are based on history, not real-time updates.

Successful investing is less about predicting the future and more about being ready for it. The best investors do not aim for perfect forecasts but, instead, prepare for uncertainty. AI can help you do exactly that. The more you use these tools thoughtfully, the more confident you will become in your decision-making. So, test your ideas, explore scenarios, and stress-test your plan. That is how you use AI, not to chase precision but to gain perspective and become a better, more resilient investor.

CHAPTER 11

PORTFOLIO CONSTRUCTION WITH AI HELP

"Diversification is the only free lunch in investing."
—*Harry Markowitz, Nobel Laureate and father of Modern Portfolio Theory*

Consider an investor who believes they are diversified because they hold dozens of different stocks, only to watch the entire portfolio decline when one sector experiences a sharp drop. That is the moment they learn that diversification is not about how many investments you own but about having a variety of investments that perform differently under different market conditions. The same lesson applies to investors in exchange-traded funds and mutual funds. Even if you own multiple funds, they may hold many of the same underlying companies, which means your portfolio may be less diversified than it appears.

Constructing a well-balanced portfolio has always been one of the cornerstones of successful investing. It is about more than just picking the right investments; rather, it is about building a collection of assets that matches your goals, fits your risk tolerance, and holds up through all kinds of markets. That sounds simple on paper, but in reality, even seasoned investors struggle with how to diversify effectively, as well as when and how to rebalance.

What Diversification Really Means

Most investors have heard the saying, "Do not put all your eggs in one basket." It is not bad advice, but it is only part of the story. True diversification is not simply owning a large number of investments but also owning the right mix of investments that respond differently when market conditions change. If you own forty technology stocks and the technology sector falls by 20%, your portfolio will still suffer a significant decline. That is some diversification, but not much. Real diversification spreads risk across sectors, asset classes, geographies, company sizes, and different economic drivers.

For example, stocks and bonds often react differently to changes in interest rates. US and international markets are influenced by different political and economic forces. Real estate and commodities may respond to inflation in ways that stocks do not. The goal is, therefore, to combine investments that do not all move in the same direction simultaneously. The challenge for most investors is determining whether their portfolio truly has that kind of diversification.

How AI Can Spot Hidden Risks

Here is where AI can help. AI is especially good at identifying relationships in complex data. One of the most useful ways it does this is by spotting correlations between assets or how closely their returns move together. If you are trying to build a portfolio that holds up in different environments, this kind of analysis is invaluable.

For example, you might think your international stock ETF adds diversification to your US holdings. However, your AI platform could point out that your international ETF is 40% invested in global technology firms, many of which are highly correlated with US technology stocks. So, you're not as diversified as you thought. Some AI-powered platforms take it a step further by analyzing what is called "factor exposure." [55] Instead of merely looking at asset classes, they examine what actually drives returns—factors like value, momentum, quality, size, and volatility. AI can help you construct a portfolio that spreads across these dimensions, not just ticker symbols.

Let's say you have a portfolio comprising the following:
- 60% US stocks (S&P 500 fund)
- 20% international stocks
- 20% bonds

This is a solid, traditional mix. However, with AI's help, you might find that nearly all your stock exposure, both US and international, is tilted toward large-cap growth. You might be missing out on small-cap value or ignoring quality and low-volatility factors that could reduce risk. AI can suggest tilts or additions, such as a small-cap value ETF or a minimum-volatility fund, to improve your overall diversification. Thus, AI does not

---

55 Factor investing means tilting your portfolio toward certain characteristics that have historically been linked to higher returns or lower risk, such as value (inexpensive stocks), size (smaller companies), or momentum (stocks that have been rising). It is a way to try to enhance performance, but it adds complexity. Most investors do not need to do factor investing to be successful because broad index funds are usually enough.

just help investors own more assets; it can help investors own the right mix of assets.

Optimizing Your Portfolio with AI

Once you have picked the right ingredients, the next question is: how much of each should you hold? This is where portfolio optimization comes into play. The goal is to find the mix of investments that either maximizes your expected return for a given level of risk or minimizes your risk for a target return. You are trying to balance growth and safety based on your unique goals, time horizon, and comfort with volatility.

Traditional portfolio theory utilizes historical averages for returns, volatility, and correlations to model risk and return. It can work reasonably well, but it is limited by the assumption that past relationships between assets will remain stable. As we know, markets are rarely that predictable. AI takes a smarter, more flexible approach that adapts as your situation or the market changes. They can process large datasets, incorporate forward-looking factors, and simulate a wider range of market scenarios, including stress events and changing economic conditions. Many of these tools allow you to set specific constraints or preferences, such as the following:

- "Cap cryptocurrency exposure at 5%."
- "Exclude fossil fuel companies."
- "Keep bond duration under seven years."

The result can be a portfolio that is not only diversified but also tailored to your goals, risk tolerance, and preferences. Platforms such as Morningstar's Portfolio Manager, Portfolio Visualizer, and Empower offer optimization and allocation analysis, with some using AI and others applying advanced algorithmic decision-making to help refine and adjust your mix. Everyday investors do not need to use these tools to be successful, but they're worth highlighting to show how AI can support smarter investing.

The Case for Rebalancing

Let's say you have built the perfect portfolio after doing your research, and it is diversified and aligned with your goals. You are done, right? Well, not quite. Over time, your portfolio will drift. Maybe tech stocks outperform for a year, and suddenly, your 60% stocks/40% bonds mix is now 70% stocks/30% bonds. Alternatively, perhaps international markets lag, shrinking their share of your portfolio. Left alone, this drift changes your risk level. It might leave you more exposed to a downturn than you realize—and this is why we rebalance.

Rebalancing is the act of trimming what has grown too large and adding to what has fallen behind, which brings your allocation back to target. It can be one of the most underappreciated disciplines in investing. Instead of relying on a rigid calendar (like rebalancing every quarter), AI can help you monitor your portfolio continuously and recommend rebalancing when it actually makes sense. That could be:

- when allocations drift beyond your chosen threshold (say, 5% or 10% off target);
- when market conditions change rapidly; or
- when there is a tax-efficient opportunity to harvest gains or losses.

Some platforms even use AI to guide the rebalancing process itself. For instance, if interest rates are rising and long-term bonds are under pressure, AI might recommend shortening bond duration or shifting to TIPS. If equity markets are volatile, it might nudge you toward more stable factor exposures like quality or low volatility.

Let's look at a real-world scenario. Suppose your target portfolio is:
- 60% stocks (40% US, 20% international),
- 30% bonds, and
- 10% real estate.

However, after a year of strong stock market performance, your portfolio now looks like the following:
- 68% stocks (48% US, 20% international);
- 25% bonds; and
- 7% real estate

An AI tool can flag this drift, show you the risk implications, and help you decide whether to:
- rebalance now;
- wait for a specific market condition; or
- gradually shift back using new contributions to your investment account(s).[56]

Previously, this kind of decision-making used to take hours or get ignored entirely. Now, it can happen in minutes, with AI doing the heavy lifting behind the scenes.

---

56 One simple way to rebalance is by directing new contributions into the parts of your portfolio that are underweight. For example, if bonds have fallen below your target allocation, you can put more of your next deposit into a bond fund until your mix is back in line. This avoids selling existing holdings and can be a tax-efficient way to get back to your target asset allocation.

Sample Portfolios Built with AI Insight

Here are three sample portfolios that demonstrate how AI can support different investment strategies. Each one is designed for a specific level of risk and return and shows how technology can tailor a portfolio to align with your goals.

Conservative Portfolio (Capital Preservation)
- 40% US Total Bond Market ETF
- 20% TIPS ETF
- 20% US Total Stock Market ETF
- 10% International Developed Market ETF
- 5% REIT ETF
- 5% AI-Selected Diversified Alternatives

This portfolio focuses on stability and income while still maintaining some growth potential. The larger allocation to bonds and TIPS is intended to reduce volatility and protect against inflation. A modest equity exposure allows for capital appreciation over time. Real estate and diversified alternatives provide additional diversification and income potential. AI monitors interest rate trends, inflation data, and sector performance. When inflation expectations rise, AI can recommend increasing TIPS exposure or adjusting REIT holdings to protect purchasing power. When volatility increases, AI can suggest shortening bond duration or shifting into higher-quality fixed income.

Balanced Portfolio (Growth with Moderate Risk)
- 35% US Total Stock Market ETF
- 20% International Developed Market ETF
- 10% International Emerging Markets ETF

- 25% US Bond ETF
- 5% REIT ETF
- 5% AI-Selected Thematic ETF (e.g., AI, clean energy, or robotics)

This portfolio seeks steady long-term growth while limiting large swings in value. A roughly equal mix of stocks and bonds provides a balance between growth and stability. While international developed markets and emerging markets offer global diversification, bonds and REITs help smooth out performance. AI evaluates economic trends, currency movements, and factor exposures to fine-tune geographic weights. Additionally, it can also identify undervalued sectors or themes, thereby adjusting the thematic ETF exposure to capture timely opportunities without disrupting the portfolio's risk profile.

Aggressive Growth Portfolio (Long-Term Appreciation)
- 55% US Total Stock Market ETF
- 20% International Emerging Markets ETF
- 10% International Developed Market ETF
- 10% AI-Enhanced ETF
- 5% Alternatives (such as cryptocurrency, venture capital, or private equity)

This portfolio prioritizes maximum long-term growth and accepts higher short-term volatility. The focus is on equities with significant exposure to emerging markets, which can deliver higher returns over time (while also carrying greater risk). AI can play a more active role here, identifying sector rotations, spotting growth themes, and signaling when to rebalance into stronger-performing areas. Besides, it can also monitor risk indicators, such as changes in market momentum or economic conditions, and recommend adjustments to reduce exposure when volatility spikes.

Case Study: Before and After AI's Help

Background

Investor A is 45 years old, has a high tolerance for risk, and is investing primarily for retirement in approximately 20 years. They manage their own portfolio, using a mix of ETFs and mutual funds. Investor A believes they are reasonably diversified and rebalances once a year using a simple calendar schedule.

Before AI

Investor A's portfolio looks like this:
- 50% US Total Stock Market ETF (VTI)
- 20% International Developed Markets ETF (VEA)
- 20% US Aggregate Bond ETF (AGG)
- 10% S&P 500 Growth ETF (IVW)[57]

Perception

Investor A thinks they have broad diversification because they own US stocks, international stocks, and bonds. They believe the additional S&P 500 Growth ETF gives them an extra boost toward growth companies.

---

57 VTI is the Vanguard Total Stock Market ETF, covering nearly the entire US equity market. VEA is the Vanguard FTSE Developed Markets ETF, which holds stocks from developed countries outside the US. AGG is the iShares Core US Aggregate Bond ETF, giving broad exposure to investment-grade US bonds. IVW is the iShares S&P 500 Growth ETF, which tracks the growth-oriented stocks within the S&P 500.

Reality

Without realizing it, Investor A has significant overlap between VTI and IVW, with many of the same top holdings. The US and international portions are both heavily tilted toward large-cap growth stocks. Bonds are all intermediate-term and concentrated in US government and agency securities. The calendar-based rebalancing sometimes causes trades in quiet markets but misses opportunities to adjust in volatile conditions.

Risks Identified

- Over 55% of total equity exposure in large-cap tech names.
- Limited factor diversification with little exposure to small-cap, value, or quality tilts.
- International allocation still correlated with US markets due to sector similarities.
- Bond allocation offers minimal inflation protection.

After AI

Investor A uses an AI-enabled portfolio analysis tool, which evaluates correlations, factor exposures, and sector concentration. It also simulates stress scenarios (e.g., rising interest rates, commodity shocks, and a tech-sector downturn) to demonstrate portfolio resilience.

Key AI Recommendations

- Reduce Redundancy: Replace the S&P 500 Growth ETF with a small-cap value ETF to improve factor balance.
- Enhance Inflation Protection: Shift 5% from AGG to a TIPS ETF to protect purchasing power.

- Improve Global Diversification: Add 5% to the emerging markets ETF by reducing the developed-market allocation, thus increasing exposure to different economic drivers.
- Dynamic Rebalancing: Switch from annual calendar re-balancing to threshold-based triggers, adjusting when allocations drift by more than 5% from target.

New Portfolio
- 45% US Total Stock Market ETF (VTI)
- 15% International Developed Markets ETF (VEA)
- 5% International Emerging Markets ETF (VWO)
- 20% US Aggregate Bond ETF (AGG)
- 5% TIPS ETF (TIP)
- 10% US Small-Cap Value ETF (VBR)[58]

Results After One Year
- Lower portfolio correlation to the S&P 500
- Reduced tech sector concentration
- Added inflation-protected fixed income without significantly lowering yield
- Maintained target risk profile while broadening diversification

Interpretation
Before AI, Investor A's portfolio appeared diversified but had hidden overlaps and factor imbalances. After AI analysis, the

---

58 VWO is the Vanguard FTSE Emerging Markets ETF, which invests in companies from developing countries such as China, India, and Brazil. TIP is the iShares TIPS Bond ETF, holding US Treasury Inflation-Protected Securities designed to guard against inflation. VBR is the Vanguard Small-Cap Value ETF, which focuses on smaller US companies trading at relatively low valuations.

portfolio became more balanced, more resilient to different market environments, and better aligned with long-term goals. AI did not replace Investor A's judgment but rather acted as a second set of eyes to identify blind spots and suggest targeted improvements.

To replicate the previous analysis for yourself, below is an example of a before-and-after prompt flow showing exactly how you could go from your starting point to an improved portfolio using only ChatGPT and freely available data.

Step 1: Baseline Portfolio Review

Investor A's Starting Prompt

Analyze my current investment portfolio:
- VTI (Vanguard Total Stock Market ETF): 50%
- VEA (Vanguard FTSE Developed Markets ETF): 20%
- AGG (iShares Core US Aggregate Bond ETF): 20%
- IVW (iShares S&P 500 Growth ETF): 10%

I am 45 years old, have high risk tolerance, and plan to retire in 20 years. My primary goal is long-term growth. Please identify my sector exposures, factor tilts, geographic diversification, and any concentration risks.

What ChatGPT Would Return (or Similar Output)

- Sector breakdown showing high technology concentration
- Factor exposure analysis showing a large-cap growth tilt with minimal small-cap or value exposure
- Geographic analysis revealing that US and international developed markets holdings have a high correlation, limiting true diversification

- Fixed income review noting all bonds are intermediate-term with limited inflation protection

Step 2: Identify Overlap

Follow-up Prompt

Calculate the percentage overlap between VTI and IVW, list the top 10 overlapping holdings, and explain how this affects diversification.

ChatGPT's Potential Output

- Overlap ~55–60% by weight, with large positions in Apple, Microsoft, Amazon, and NVIDIA.
- Conclusion: This overlap does not add significant diversification and increases concentration risk.

Step 3: Suggest Adjustments

Follow-up Prompt

Based on my profile, recommend portfolio adjustments to reduce concentration risk, improve factor diversification, and add inflation protection. Keep overall volatility similar to my current portfolio.

ChatGPT's Potential Output

- Replace IVW with VBR (US small-cap value ETF) to balance growth and value exposure.
- Shift 5% of AGG into TIP (TIPS ETF) for inflation protection.

- Reallocate 5% from VEA into VWO (emerging markets ETF) to add exposure to different economic drivers.

Step 4: Rebalancing Strategy

Follow-up Prompt

Design a rebalancing strategy that triggers adjustments only when allocations drift more than 5% from target. Provide rules for monitoring and suggested tools to track this.

ChatGPT's Potential Output

- A clear threshold-based rebalancing plan that reduces unnecessary trades
- Recommendations for using free tools like Portfolio Visualizer or Morningstar Portfolio Manager to monitor drift

Step 5: Final Portfolio and Rationale

Final Prompt

Present my new portfolio with target allocations and explain how it improves diversification, factor exposure, and inflation protection compared to my starting point.

ChatGPT's Potential Output

New Portfolio
- 45% VTI
- 15% VEA
- 5% VWO
- 20% AGG

- 5% TIP
- 10% VBR

Benefits
- Reduced technology sector concentration
- Added small-cap value exposure to diversify factors
- Increased inflation protection
- Broader geographic diversification with meaningful emerging markets allocation

Example AI Prompts for Portfolio Management

Consider trying some of these prompts in AI-enabled investing tools like Morningstar Mo, Portfolio Visualizer, ChatGPT, or others as appropriate for your own portfolio:

- "Calculate the exact correlation between my three largest holdings (list holdings) over the past five years and suggest adjustments if the correlation exceeds 0.80."
- "Recommend three ETFs that specifically reduce concentration risk from my largest holdings (list your top holdings or sectors) while keeping similar expected returns."
- "Run a detailed simulation to show how adding a 10% allocation to a highly rated, low-cost gold ETF would affect both the annual volatility and cumulative performance of my portfolio over the past 20 years."
- "Suggest a specific bond allocation strategy or ETFs to help reduce my portfolio's duration risk, especially if interest rates continue rising over the next two years."
- "Identify the top three sectors where my current portfolio (list holdings or tickers) is significantly underweight relative to the S&P 500 and recommend ETFs to address these gaps."

- "Measure the percentage overlap between my holdings in VTI and QQQ. Suggest alternative ETFs if the overlap exceeds 50% to maintain broad exposure with less redundancy."
- "Design a portfolio allocation using factor-based diversification (momentum, value, quality, low volatility) tailored specifically to my risk tolerance (moderate or aggressive) and long-term goals."
- "Quantify how shifting from my bond ETF BND to short-term Treasury ETFs would change my interest rate risk, overall volatility, and expected income over the next five years."
- "Show the projected dollar impact on my portfolio if stocks decline by 20% and suggest adjustments to cushion against large drawdowns, given my current allocation (list current asset mix)."
- "List three low-cost ETFs that provide strong exposure to small-cap value stocks, enhancing diversification in my current equity portfolio."
- "Provide a list of thematic ETFs (e.g., clean energy, AI, and robotics) that have historically low correlation (under 0.50) to my existing portfolio holdings (list your current largest positions)."
- "Identify specific holdings in my portfolio (list tickers and cost basis) that currently have unrealized losses suitable for immediate tax-loss harvesting and suggest similar ETFs for reinvestment."
- "Given current macroeconomic trends, recommend the maximum reasonable international equity exposure for my portfolio without introducing excessive risk."
- "Analyze whether adding a 10–15% allocation to REIT ETFs would meaningfully increase my portfolio's income

and diversification and suggest appropriate ETFs to achieve this."

- "Suggest three ESG-focused ETFs with comparable historical risk/return profiles to my current core holdings (list your core ETFs or funds) to integrate sustainable investing without sacrificing performance."[59]
- "Analyze my current portfolio's allocation and quantify deviations from a target 70% stocks/30% bonds split. Recommend specific ETF adjustments to realign with this goal."
- "Break down the contribution of each holding (list holdings) to overall portfolio volatility and highlight any securities disproportionately increasing risk."
- "Optimize my existing portfolio for the lowest possible drawdown risk over the next decade, including suggested allocations to defensive asset classes or ETFs."
- "Highlight specific hidden sector or factor biases in my portfolio (list holdings) that I may not have noticed and provide ETF recommendations to correct any imbalances."
- "Compare my current portfolio allocation to a target-date 2045 fund, pinpoint differences in asset allocation or risk, and propose actionable changes to better align my holdings with my retirement timeline."
- "Based on a moderate risk profile, suggest an appropriate percentage allocation to cryptocurrency and recommend the safest ETF options available to gain this exposure."
- "Create a specific globally diversified ETF portfolio allocation with a combined weighted-average expense ratio below 0.10%, covering stocks, bonds, and real assets."

---

59 Environmental, Social, and Governance (ESG) investing means choosing funds, including ETFs, that focus on companies that aim to be sustainable, treat people fairly, and follow strong governance practices.

- "Based on the historical volatility of the major asset classes in my portfolio, recommend exactly how often (annually, semi-annually, quarterly) I should rebalance to maintain optimal risk-adjusted returns."

The best portfolios are the ones you truly understand and can stick with through market ups and downs. AI can make your investing approach more efficient and less driven by emotion. Moreover, it can process the data, point out blind spots, and offer helpful suggestions. Remember, AI can help you fine-tune your portfolio, but discipline is what keeps it growing over time.

CHAPTER 12

RETHINKING RETIREMENT

"The question isn't at what age I want to retire; it's at what income."
—*George Foreman*

Retirement is not about having a certain number of candles on your birthday cake, nor is it about turning 65 years old or qualifying for Medicare. Retirement is about reaching the point where your investment accounts can support your lifestyle without needing a paycheck. It is a financial milestone, not an age-based one. For decades, the idea of retirement has been tied to age, but that is changing. Today, some people retire at 55 years old, while others work well into their 70s—some because they want to, others because they have to. The real issue is not when you retire but whether you can afford to retire and stay retired. Put simply, retirement is when work becomes optional.

Retirement Is Still One of the Most Common Financial Goals

Ask most people what they are saving for, and retirement will usually be on top of their lists. It is not just about quitting your job but also about freedom and flexibility. Some people want to travel, while others want to spend more time with their grandkids. There may even be some who want to golf three times a week or volunteer at a local nonprofit. No matter the dream, retirement gives you the time to pursue what matters most to you. However, achieving that dream takes planning. You will not wake up one day and find that you are magically set. Retirement success is built through consistent saving, smart investing, and thoughtful trade-offs.

Are You on Track?

Most people do not want to live a life where they have to work just to pay the bills. Retirement planning is about buying your time back. To give you a general sense of how you are doing, below are some retirement savings benchmarks by age based on a multiple of your salary. Note that these are meant as guidelines, not hard rules, and they assume you want to retire by age 67 with enough saved to replace 80–90% of your pre-retirement income.

Retirement Savings Benchmarks by Age

Target = Combined Investment Account Balances as a Multiple of Salary[60]

---

[60] Source: Fidelity Investments—Retirement Savings Guidelines (https://www.fidelity.com/viewpoints/retirement/how-much-do-i-need-to-retire). Fidelity's model assumes you start saving early, typically around age 25, and contribute about 15% of your pre-tax income each year, including any employer match. Those savings are invested in a portfolio

Age	Recommended Savings
30	1× salary
35	2× salary
40	3× salary
45	4× salary
50	6× salary
55	7× salary
60	8× salary
67	10× salary

So, if you make $80,000 a year, by age 50, you would want to have around $480,000 saved. At age 60, you would aim for $640,000. These are just ballpark targets, but they give you a solid reference point. You can always adjust up or down based on your spending habits and retirement lifestyle goals.

How AI Can Help You Plan for Retirement

Many people do not have access to a financial advisor. However, they now have something powerful at their fingertips: AI. AI cannot replace judgment or personalized financial advice, but it can help you in the following:
- Run projections and simulate different retirement dates

---

that is at least 50% stocks over your working years. The guideline targets you toward saving 10× your salary by age 67 if you plan to replace roughly 45% of your pre-retirement income with savings, with the rest coming from Social Security. The projections assume you plan to live until about age 93–94, use a safe initial withdrawal rate of 4–5%, and see inflation at around 2.5% annually, with all income, expenses, and benefits adjusted accordingly.

- Estimate how much you will need based on your lifestyle
- Evaluate tradeoffs like retiring early versus working longer
- Choose the best time to claim Social Security for maximum benefit
- Model tax-smart withdrawals, Roth conversions, and required distributions
- Track your spending and suggest adjustments
- Build a clear withdrawal plan that balances taxes and long-term growth

Furthermore, AI can answer questions such as the following:
- "How much can I withdraw each year without running out of money?"
- "Should I convert my IRA to a Roth before age 73?"
- "How does delaying Social Security affect my long-term wealth when I balance higher future benefits against giving up income now?"

In short, AI can take the guesswork out of your retirement planning and give you more assurance in the decisions you are making.

Retirement Basics

Let's walk through the key steps for those who want to focus on retirement planning:

Step 1: Know How Much You Need

You cannot plan for retirement if you do not know your target. One simple rule of thumb is the 25x rule: multiply your expected annual retirement expenses by 25. Your annual retirement expenses should cover everything you will need to live comfortably (housing, food, healthcare, insurance, travel, fun money, etc.). Be sure to also include things that come up less often, like home repairs or gifts for family. If you will need $80,000 per year, you should aim for $2 million in investable assets (25 x $80,000). That's based on the idea that a 4% withdrawal rate is generally sustainable for a 30-year retirement.[61] But that is just a starting point. AI can tailor this estimate based on your actual expenses, life expectancy, portfolio mix, and expected Social Security income.

Step 2: Save Early, Save Consistently

Time matters. The earlier you start saving and investing, the more compound growth works in your favor. Even if you can only save a few hundred dollars a month, it adds up over decades. Therefore, make saving automatic. Use workplace retirement plans (401(k), 403(b)) and individual retirement accounts (IRAs or Roth IRAs) to your advantage. Be sure to maximize any employer match when it's offered because it's essentially free money.

Step 3: Don't Just Save, Invest

Keeping money in a savings account probably will not get you to retirement. You need assets that grow over time, like stocks, mutual funds, or ETFs. A diversified portfolio aligned to your

---

61 Withdrawal rates describe how much of your portfolio you take out each year in retirement. The well-known "4% rule" was based on research suggesting that starting with a 4% withdrawal rate could make savings last about 30 years. Today, some experts suggest aiming closer to 3 - 3.5% unless you can adjust spending when markets are down.

goals and risk tolerance is key. During your working years, that likely means more stocks for growth, and as you get closer to retirement, you may shift to less volatile investments. AI can help evaluate your asset mix, rebalance it periodically, and even flag unnecessary risk.

Step 4: Plan for Inflation

If you need $70,000 per year today, you will need closer to $115,000 in 20 years, assuming 2.5% inflation. Thus, your plan needs to grow not just to meet your current expenses but also your future ones. This is why growth-oriented assets, particularly in the early stages of retirement, remain important.

Step 5: Account for Healthcare

Medicare does not cover everything. You will still have premiums, deductibles, prescriptions, dental, vision, and possibly long-term care needs. AI can help you estimate healthcare costs year by year and explore options like supplemental plans or HSAs while you are still working.

Step 6: Know Your Income Sources

You will likely draw income from multiple places. Examples may include the following:
- Social Security;
- IRAs, 401(k)s, and Roth accounts;
- taxable brokerage accounts;

- pensions;
- part-time work; and
- real estate rental income.

Knowing what is coming in and when it starts helps build a clear drawdown strategy, something AI can help you optimize.

Example: A Retired Couple Using AI For Help

Let's look at a detailed example.

Meet John and Karen

- John is 68, and Karen is 66.
- They retired last year and want to live comfortably and leave something to their kids.
- They expect to spend around $85,000 per year after taxes.
- Their house is paid off, and they want to travel for the next 10 years.

Assets

Account	Balance
John's 401(k)	$950,000
Karen's 403(b)	$800,000
Roth IRAs (combined)	$250,000
Taxable Brokerage	$350,000
Cash	$75,000
Total	$2.425 million

Income
- Social Security:
  - o   John receives $3,000 per month.
  - o   Karen receives $2,100 per month.
- Combined = $61,200 per year
- No pensions

Example Prompt with Output and Interpretation

Prompt
"Are we on track to maintain $85,000 per year in spending adjusted for 30 years?"

AI Output
Yes. Based on your current portfolio value, inflation-adjusted withdrawals of $85,000 annually are sustainable with a 93% success rate, assuming 5% investment returns and 2.5% inflation. To increase your margin, consider reducing withdrawals slightly after age 85 or shifting more to Roth to reduce future taxes.

Prompt
"Should we take Roth withdrawals now or wait?"

AI Output
With your Social Security covering about 70% of your expenses, withdrawals from Roth IRAs can help reduce your taxable income in early retirement. Suggest splitting withdrawals: 60% from pre-tax and 40% from

Roth to smooth your tax liability and reduce RMDs later.

Prompt
"How can we plan for RMDs starting at age 73?"

AI Output
RMDs from your traditional accounts are projected to start at approximately $75,000 combined in the first year. Consider Roth conversions now to reduce future RMDs. Converting $50,000 per year from 2025 to 2027 would keep you in the 22% bracket and reduce RMDs by approximately 25%.

Prompt
"We want to gift $10,000 per year to each of our two grandchildren. Is that tax-efficient?"

AI Output
Yes. In 2025, the annual gift exclusion is $18,000 per donor, per recipient. You can each give $10,000 to each grandchild without filing a gift tax return. Consider contributing to their 529 plans or custodial Roth IRAs if they have earned income.

Interpretation
John and Karen used AI to help them get a handle on their financial picture and confirm they were on track. With a total of $2.425 million in assets and about $61,000 a year from Social Security, they wanted to know if they could safely spend $85,000 annually and make it through a 30-year retirement. AI crunched

the numbers and gave them the green light, showing a high probability of success, especially if they made a few small adjustments.

An important suggestion they received was to use a mix of traditional and Roth withdrawals. Tapping into both types of accounts is a smart way to handle taxes throughout retirement. By doing this, they can manage their taxable income to stay in a lower bracket and reduce the future tax burden from RMDs on their traditional accounts.

Looking ahead, AI pointed out that their RMDs would begin at age 73 and could be significant. To stay in a favorable tax bracket, it recommended converting some of their traditional assets to Roth IRAs over the next few years. John and Karen also wanted to give $10,000 annually to each grandchild, which the AI platform confirmed could be done tax-free and provided suggestions on how to do it. Overall, the couple walked away with a clear, tax-aware strategy to maintain their lifestyle, support their family, and manage their retirement income wisely.

AI Prompts for Retirement-Focused Individuals and Families

Social Security
- "What is my break-even age for delaying Social Security?"
- "How does my benefit change if I claim at age 62, 67, or 70?"
- "If I am married, what's the best claiming strategy for both spouses?"

Roth Conversions and Tax Planning

- "How much can I convert to Roth this year without hitting the 24% tax bracket?"
- "Should I do Roth conversions before my RMDs start?"
- "What's the long-term tax impact of converting $50,000 per year for five years?"
- "Can I avoid Income-Related Monthly Adjustment Amount (IRMAA) Medicare surcharges by spreading conversions?"

RMDs and Withdrawals

- "When do RMDs begin, and how are they calculated?"
- "What is the projected tax liability from my RMDs?"
- "Should I use qualified charitable distributions (QCDs) from my IRA to satisfy RMDs and reduce taxes?"

Asset Location and Order of Withdrawals

- "Which account should I draw from first: Roth, traditional, or taxable?"
- "How can I minimize taxes while meeting my income needs?"
- "Run a withdrawal order analysis for the next 20 years."

Healthcare and Long-Term Care

- "Estimate my Medicare costs with and without a supplemental plan."
- "What's the average cost of assisted living in my area?"
- "Can I self-fund long-term care without insurance?"

Gifting and Legacy

- "What is the most tax-efficient way to leave money to my kids?"

- "Should I set up a trust or leave assets outright?"
- "How do SECURE Act[62] rules affect inherited IRAs?"
- "Create a gifting plan using the annual gift tax exclusion and 529 plan superfunding."

Retirement Modeling and Planning

- "Run a retirement simulation assuming $80,000 in annual withdrawals, adjusted for 2.5% inflation over 30 years. Assume a starting portfolio of $3 million and a 60% stocks/40% bonds asset allocation. Show the probability of success and suggest any adjustments needed to improve sustainability."
- "Re-run my retirement simulation but assume inflation averages 3.5% instead of 2.5%."
- "How much can I spend annually during retirement and still leave $500,000 to my kids?"
- "What is the impact of a market downturn in the first five years of retirement?"

Lifestyle and Housing

- "Should I downsize and invest the equity or stay in my current home?"
- "Can I afford a second home or extended travel in retirement?"
- "What is the trade-off of working part-time until 70?"

---

62 The SECURE Act (Setting Every Community Up for Retirement Enhancement Act) changed how inherited IRAs work. Most non-spouse beneficiaries now must withdraw the full balance within 10 years of the original owner's death, rather than stretching distributions over their lifetime. Spouses, certain minors, and disabled or chronically ill beneficiaries may still qualify for exceptions. These rules apply to IRAs inherited after 2019 and they can significantly affect tax timing and planning strategies.

Advanced Scenarios

- "Create a Roth conversion ladder strategy that starts before age 59½, including any tax or penalty considerations."
- "Model my net worth over time using variable withdrawal rates that adjust for portfolio returns and inflation."
- "Evaluate the tax benefit of bunching charitable contributions every other year."

Retirement does not begin at a specific age. It begins when you have enough financial resources to stop working because you want to, not because you have to. The real goal is freedom. That might mean traveling, spending time with family, giving back to your community, or simply enjoying each day without the pressure of needing a paycheck. AI will not replace thoughtful planning, but it can make the process clearer and more manageable. Moreover, it can help you test different scenarios, explore trade-offs, and make better-informed decisions along the way. Retirement is about having control over your time and the ability to live life on your own terms. That kind of freedom comes from planning ahead and making thoughtful decisions now, as well as along the way.

CHAPTER 13

PUTTING EVERYTHING TOGETHER

*"Planning is bringing the future into the present
so you can do something about it now."*
—*Alan Lakein*

Most people know they should have a financial plan. However, knowing and doing are two vastly different things. The truth is that building a financial plan can feel overwhelming, especially when you are unsure where to start or, worse, afraid of what you might find. But it does not have to be that way.

This chapter aims to provide you with a step-by-step framework to build a real, usable financial plan—one that connects your goals with your money and puts you in control of your future. We will utilize AI to make the process easier, faster, and far more approachable. If you have ever said, "I don't have time to build a plan" or "I don't know where to begin," this chapter is for you.

Step 1: Set Clear Financial Goals

Every plan starts with one or more goals. These can be short-term, medium-term, or long-term goals, but they need to be specific and meaningful to you. Ask yourself the following questions:

- What does financial success look like for you?
- What do you want to accomplish in the next one, five, and 20 years?
- What is your ideal life, and what role does money play in it?

As discussed previously, common financial goals may include the following:

- Paying off debt
- Buying a home
- Starting a business
- Funding college for your children
- Retirement

With your goals in hand, you can prompt AI and ask for help in building around them.

Financial Goal Sample Prompts

- "I have a list of personal goals, such as buying a home, retiring early, and traveling more. Help me rewrite each one as a SMART financial goal with specific timelines, measurable targets, and dollar amounts where possible."
- "I am 40 years old and want to retire by the age of 55. My dream is to travel for approximately three months each year in retirement. Based on that lifestyle, estimate how

much I would need to save annually starting now and what kind of investment return I would need to assume."

- "Create a prioritized financial plan for someone who wants to buy a $400,000 home in three years, currently has $30,000 in student loans with a 5% interest rate, earns $85,000 per year, and wants to start investing for retirement. Include savings goals, a debt payoff strategy, and suggested investment contributions."

Use the output to refine your goals into something you can measure and plan against.

Step 2: Analyze Your Cash Flow

Before you can invest, you need to understand your income and expenses. This is where most people stall. Fortunately, AI can help you categorize, summarize, and optimize your cash flow faster than you could on your own. You can copy and paste in bank transactions or summarize recent expenses and ask AI to help you break them down.

Cash Flow Sample Prompts
- Here is a list of my monthly expenses (include amounts and descriptions). Help me sort them into fixed (e.g., rent and insurance), variable (e.g., utilities and groceries), and discretionary (e.g., dining out and subscriptions) categories. Then, based on average spending in each category, show me where I might be overspending and suggest realistic ways to cut back."
- "I earn $7,500 per month after taxes. My rent is $2,000, and I estimate spending $3,500 on everything else (i.e.,

groceries, transportation, and dining, among others). Based on this, how much can I realistically invest each month while still leaving enough buffer for unexpected expenses or lifestyle flexibility? Suggest both a conservative and a more aggressive option."

- "Help me create a monthly budget using percentage allocations. Suggest a sample breakdown (with percentages and dollar amounts) for someone earning $6,000 per month after taxes. I want to
  o   save 20% for short-term goals/emergencies;
  o   invest 15% for long-term growth;
  o   cover all essential expenses; and
  o   still have enough left for discretionary spending like travel or dining."

Once you have a clear sense of your spending and saving capacity, you can start mapping your dollars to your goals.

Step 3: Build Your Investment Strategy

This is where most people want to start. However, without clear goals and a cash flow analysis, investing becomes random. The key is to build an investment strategy aligned with your timeline and risk tolerance.

Three Core Questions
- What is this money for? (Goal-based investing)
- How long do I have before I need it? (Time horizon)
- How comfortable am I with ups and downs? (Risk tolerance)

AI can guide you through this process and suggest portfolio allocations based on your profile. It can also summarize fund choices, compare mutual funds/ETFs, and help you avoid high-fee or redundant investments.

Investment Sample Prompts

- "I am 35 years old, planning to retire by the age of 60, and have a moderate risk tolerance. I currently have no major debts and contribute regularly to a 401(k) and Roth IRA. Based on this, what asset allocation would you recommend across stocks and bonds? Include a breakdown by asset class (e.g., US versus international markets and large cap versus small cap) and explain why it fits someone with my profile."
- "I am a long-term, buy-and-hold investor looking for a total US stock market ETF with very low fees, strong tracking accuracy, and broad diversification. Please compare the top ETFs that meet this criterion. Which is the most cost-efficient and ideal for a passive investor?"
- "Help me build a globally diversified portfolio for someone in their 20s, using mostly stocks and a smaller portion of bonds. Keep the choices simple and low cost with ETFs. Include US stocks, international market funds, and a mix of US and global bonds. Show me the specific ETFs, their tickers, and how much to put in each."

From there, you can optionally plug your chosen allocation into a tool like Portfolio Visualizer or Morningstar's portfolio analysis platform to review historical performance, risk metrics, and potential outcomes.

Step 4: Evaluate Risk and Insurance Needs

Risk is not just about how volatile your portfolio is but about what could derail your plan (e.g., job loss, disability, market downturns, or unexpected expenses). AI can help you model these risks and even compare insurance options.

You can use AI to walk through the following:

- emergency fund targets,
- life and disability insurance needs,
- job loss impact scenarios, and
- withdrawal sequence risk in retirement.

Risk and Insurance Sample Prompts

- "Assume I lose my job and my monthly expenses are $3,000. I have a $15,000 emergency fund. How many months would that cover, and what specific spending cuts or temporary changes could help me stretch it further without sacrificing essentials like housing, food, or insurance?"
- "I am single with no dependents and have $100,000 in student loans. Most of the loans are federal, but some are private. Do I need life insurance, or are there cases where it still makes sense to have coverage? Please explain how the type of loan, co-signers, or my future plans might affect the decision."[63]

---

63 Life insurance usually makes sense when someone depends on your income. If you are single with no dependents, you probably do not need it yet, especially if your student loans are federal since they are discharged if you pass away. Private loans can be different, especially if they have a co-signer who would be on the hook. In that case, a small term life insurance policy can be a simple way to protect them until the debt is paid off.

- "Please compare 20-year-term life insurance policies with $500,000 in coverage from three top-rated insurers. Include premiums for a healthy 35-year-old non-smoker, financial strength ratings, optional riders (like disability waiver or accelerated death benefits), and any differences in customer service or claims reputation."

Moreover, you can use AI to run stress tests and ensure you are not building a beautiful plan on a shaky foundation.

Step 5: Build a Tracking System You Will Actually Use

Even the best plan will not help if you do not track progress. However, that does not mean you need to check your net worth every day. Instead, build a system using AI that checks key metrics regularly and surfaces what needs attention.

You can use tools like the following:
- Personal finance dashboards like Tiller or YNAB[64]
- Monthly AI summaries of spending, savings, and investment performance

Financial Tracking Sample Prompts
- "Based on my checking, savings, and credit card balances, along with my categorized spending (e.g., housing, groceries, dining, and travel), and current investment holdings, create a detailed monthly financial summary. Include the following:
  o Total income and expenses
  o Spending breakdown by category

---

64 YNAB stands for "You Need a Budget." It is a popular personal finance app.

o Month-over-month change in savings and net worth
o Investment performance (gains/losses and % change)"

- "Compare my spending for the current month to the previous month by category. Show percentage increases or decreases for major areas like housing, transportation, food, entertainment, and subscriptions. Highlight any categories where spending increased by more than 15% or dropped significantly. Additionally, note any new recurring charges or canceled subscriptions."

- "Track my discretionary spending categories like dining out, shopping, entertainment, and travel against the monthly budgets I set. Alert me at the end of each week if I exceed my planned budget in any category by more than 10%. Include the amount over budget and suggest where I might rebalance or cut back to stay on track."

Think of AI as your personal CFO that, instead of nagging you, makes it easy to see what is working and what needs tweaking.

Financial Plan Sample Built with AI

This is an example of what a personalized financial plan might look like when built using AI and real data. You can use a combination of ChatGPT for decision support, Tiller for automated budgeting, and Portfolio Visualizer for investment analysis.

The Smith Family Financial Plan
Goals
- Pay off $15,000 in student loans within four years.
- Save $50,000 for a home down payment within five years.

- Reach $2 million in retirement savings by age 60 to support a future income of $70,000 per year in today's dollars.

Cash Flow Summary
- Net monthly income: $8,000
- Fixed and variable expenses: $5,200
- Target savings rate: 35%
- Monthly savings/investments: $2,800
  - o $1,500 toward Roth IRA + brokerage
  - o $1,000 into high-yield savings for house down payment
  - o $300 toward student loan payoff

Investment Plan
- Asset Allocation: 80% stocks/20% bonds (moderate-aggressive):
  ETFs used:
  - o VTI (US total market stocks)
  - o VXUS (International stocks)
  - o BND (US aggregate bonds)
- All expense ratios under 0.05%
- Portfolio reviewed and rebalanced quarterly using Portfolio Visualizer

Risk Management
- Emergency Fund: $25,000 (covers five months of expenses)
- Term Life Insurance: $400,000, 20-year term, $28/month
- Disability Insurance: Covered through employer benefits
- Health Insurance: Through spouse's employer

Tracking and Review
Monthly:
- Automated budget and net worth tracking using Tiller-connected Google Sheets

- Optional: AI-generated summaries or alerts via custom ChatGPT scripts or Excel/Sheets add-ons (e.g., notifications for overspending, missed contributions, or savings milestones)

Quarterly:
- Review portfolio performance against your target allocation (use tools like Portfolio Visualizer or Morningstar).
- Analyze savings rate and spending trends compared to your goals.

Annually:
- Reassess your financial goals, insurance coverage, and retirement progress.
- Update your assumptions (income, expenses, investment returns, etc.).
- Adjust your plan as needed based on life changes.

Your Turn: Build Your Own Plan Using These AI Prompts

Use the examples below to start customizing your own plan. These prompts are designed to help you work through each section using AI tools step by step. You can mix, match, and modify them based on your income, goals, and preferences. To get the most helpful and accurate guidance, make sure to enter your own goals, income, and spending details so the AI can tailor its recommendations to you.

Goals
- "Rewrite my top five financial goals as SMART goals with specific timelines, dollar amounts, and measurable milestones."

- "Estimate how much I need to retire at age 60 if I want $75,000 per year in inflation-adjusted income. Include assumptions like investment returns, Social Security, and lifespan."

Cash Flow

- "Analyze my monthly income of $6,500 and this list of expenses (include your expenses). Summarize my spending by category and identify three realistic areas to cut back so I can increase my savings rate."
- "Create a flexible 50/30/20 budget using a $6,500/month income. Account for months where income or expenses may vary and suggest how to smooth my cash flow."

Investing

- "Based on a goal to retire at age 60 and a moderate risk tolerance, create a long-term investment strategy that includes target asset allocation, suggested account types (e.g., Roth IRA, 401(k), brokerage), and monthly contribution amounts. Prioritize low-cost, diversified ETFs and explain how the mix supports both growth and stability over time."
- "Compare three 2065 target-date funds (e.g., from Vanguard, Fidelity, and Schwab) based on asset allocation, fees, glide path, and past performance."

Risk Management

- "Stress test my financial plan by simulating a job loss or income interruption for six months. Show how my emergency fund would hold up and what changes I should make to stay on track."
- "Evaluate my current insurance coverage (health, disability, renters/homeowners, auto) and identify any

major gaps or overlaps based on my income, assets, and responsibilities."

Tracking and Review

*   "Help me build a Google Sheet to track my income, expenses, savings rate, and investment balances each month. Include charts and automatic summaries where possible."
*   "List the 3–5 key financial metrics I should review every quarter to stay aligned with my goals. Include elements like savings rate, investment returns, net worth changes, and budget variances."

A financial plan, whether built with AI or with a traditional advisor, is only useful if you actually put it into action. One of the biggest advantages of using AI to build a financial plan is how quickly and easily you can get started. With just a few prompts, you can walk away with a rough plan in minutes. It can be tailored to your age, goals, income, and risk tolerance. Moreover, it helps you prioritize, test different scenarios, and connect the dots between your spending, saving, investing, and long-term goals. For anyone who has delayed planning because it felt expensive or too complicated, AI helps remove those barriers and puts powerful tools within reach.

That said, even the best financial plan does not work like a crystal ball. Life changes, markets fluctuate, and no tool can fully account for your emotional responses to risk, uncertainty, or opportunity. Your plan only works if you actually use it, not if it hides in a folder somewhere. While AI is excellent at organizing information and offering next steps, it cannot replace action on your part. It does not matter if your plan comes from AI or a professional because the real value is in following through, reviewing it often, and making changes as your circumstances evolve.

A thoughtful financial plan provides a framework for making better choices and a benchmark to measure your progress. AI can make that process faster and a lot less intimidating. The best financial plan is one you understand, believe in, and actually use.

CHAPTER 14

LET AI BE YOUR SECOND SET OF EYES

*"The investor's chief problem—and even his worst enemy—
is likely to be himself."*
—Benjamin Graham

Charles Ellis, in *Winning the Loser's Game*, correctly compares investing to tennis. In this sport, unforced errors hurt the most, as they are self-inflicted. Investing is no different. Most investors are derailed not by market crashes but by panic selling, market timing, chasing trends, ignoring fees, and so on. While you cannot control the market, you can control your decisions. The goal is not to hit the perfect shot every time but to stay in the game and avoid beating yourself.

You do not need to be a professional money manager to be a good investor, but you do need to avoid making misguided decisions with your money. Most investing mistakes do not stem from a lack of intelligence but from emotional responses or the absence of a solid plan, to name just two. Successful investing ultimately comes down to a few core habits: staying diversified, being consistent, minimizing fees and taxes, and committing to the long haul.

Below are 10 common and costly mistakes investors tend to make if they are not careful, along with tips on how to side-step them.

1. Not Having a Plan

Let's start with the most obvious yet often overlooked problem: a lack of a solid investment plan. Many people begin investing simply because they feel they should. Hoping to retire early or set money aside for the unexpected, they open a brokerage account, pick a few mutual funds they heard about, and buy a couple of stocks. This is not a plan. A good plan should answer the following key questions:

- Why are you investing in the first place?
- What are your time horizons?
- How much risk can you handle without losing sleep?
- What mix of assets aligns with your goals?

If you enter the investing arena without clear answers to these questions, every market dip will feel like a crisis, and every headline will become a reason to second-guess yourself.

2. Trying to Time the Market

This one is tempting. We all think we can sell right before a market crash and buy right before the rebound. However, timing the market is a fool's game. Here is what usually happens: the market drops unexpectedly, and investors say, "I'm going to wait until things settle down." Then, it rebounds before they can get back in. Besides missing the drop, they miss the recovery too, which is when most gains occur. Study after study shows that the average investor underperforms the market, not because they chose bad investments but because they jumped in and out at the wrong times.[65] A better approach would be to focus on *time in* the market, not *timing* the market.

3. Letting Emotions Drive Decisions

Fear tends to surface when markets drop. You may find yourself checking your portfolio more often and feeling unsettled by the red numbers. Greed can show up when markets are soaring. You hear stories of people making big money in stocks, cryptocurrencies, or whatever is trending, and it is hard not to feel like you are missing out. However, that urge to jump in can be just as risky as panic selling. The challenge is not to eliminate these emotions but to learn how to recognize them and avoid getting caught up in the frenzy. Skilled investors understand that managing emotions is just as challenging as managing their portfolio.

4. Overconcentration in One Stock or Sector

Sometimes, you start small, and one investment takes off. You let it run, and before long, it dominates your portfolio. Or perhaps your job, paycheck, and stock options are all tied to the same company or industry. That's a big bet on one result.

---

65 Many studies have been conducted on this subject. Professor Burton Malkiel has written extensively about it. A popular personal finance investing text that addresses this is Malkiel, B. G. (2023). A Random Walk Down Wall Street: The Time-Tested Strategy for Successful Investing (13th ed.).

Diversification may not feel exciting, but it is what keeps a setback from becoming a disaster. You do not need to own everything, just enough variety across sectors and asset types to avoid betting on one thing. If you have a significant position in one stock, ensure the rest of your plan helps balance that out.

5. Ignoring Fees and Expenses

This one is easy to miss because it does not feel urgent. A 1% fee does not sound like much, but over time, it can add up and reduce your returns.

M1.com ran the calculations and wrote about it.[66] If you invest $10,000 and earn 7% per year for 30 years, you'll end up with about $76,000, assuming annual fees of 0.5%. Increase those fees to 1.5% and that drops to approximately $60,000. That is a $16,000 difference just from one extra percentage point in fees. It is not just expense ratios, either. Transaction costs, front-end loads, and high-turnover strategies that trigger taxes all eat away at performance. The good news? Low-cost index funds and ETFs make it easy to invest efficiently. Fees are one of the few aspects you can control, and they matter more than most people think.

6. Chasing Performance

Everyone wants to own the top-performing stock or the hottest fund, so it is easy to chase whatever did well last year. However, by the time something gets discussed because of its phenomenal performance, the big gains may already be behind it. A smarter approach is to choose investments that fit your plan and risk

---

66 "Understanding Investment Fees: Long-Term Impact on Returns," M1.com, December 2024.

tolerance, not just what is trending. Even great funds have off years, and selling too quickly often does more harm than good.

7. Not Rebalancing

Markets move, and that is a good thing because it may mean your investments are growing. However, over time, your portfolio can drift. As discussed previously, if stocks outperform for a few years, your initial stock allocation percentage could be higher than you are aiming for, resulting in taking more risk than you planned. Rebalancing means adjusting your portfolio by trimming what has grown and adding to what has lagged, so you stay aligned with your plan. It may feel counterintuitive, but it helps manage risk. Do it on a set schedule or when your portfolio drifts significantly.

8. Misunderstanding Risk Tolerance

Most people think they can handle more risk than they actually can. Can you stay invested during a bear market? How soon will you need the money? If your portfolio does not match your true tolerance, you may panic sell during volatile markets. It is better to take a little less risk and stay invested than to take too much and panic sell.

9. Overtrading

More trading can lead to more mistakes. The more you trade, the more you may pay in taxes (when selling winners without tax-loss harvesting). Additionally, you also lose out on compound growth when gains get taxed early. Most investors are better off building a low-cost, diversified portfolio and checking it a few times a year.

10. Not Investing at All

Finally, one of the biggest mistakes is sitting on the sidelines. Some people are so afraid of losing money that they never start. Others wait for the perfect moment to invest while inflation quietly chips away at their cash. The market has delivered positive returns over time through wars, recessions, and uncertainty. Time is your best advantage. Starting early means you can save less each month and still reach your goals, while waiting can become one of the costliest financial choices you can make.

Using AI to Help Avoid Common Investing Mistakes

Using AI to avoid common investing mistakes is a practical way to improve your decision-making. Most investors do not fall short because of a lack of knowledge but because they slip into familiar traps. AI can help you slow down, run the numbers, and make more informed choices. Whether you are stress-testing your portfolio, comparing investment approaches, or checking if a move aligns with your goals, the right prompt can keep you from making costly errors. Below are a few examples of prompts and how they can help.

Planning and Alignment
Addresses the Mistake: Not Having a Plan
- "Compare my current holdings, contribution schedule, and risk level with my stated goals and suggest where I may have drifted."

- "Recommend how my asset allocation should shift over time as I approach retirement, based on my current age, goals, and risk tolerance."
- "Show how gradually increasing my monthly contributions by 1–2% each year could improve my long-term financial position."

Staying Invested Instead of Chasing the Perfect Moment
Addresses the Mistake: Trying to Time the Market

- "Estimate the performance drag from missing just a few of the best days in the market over time."
- "Based on historical data and current market conditions, evaluate which approach (lump-sum investing or dollar-cost averaging) is more appropriate for my upcoming cash investment."
- "I have been holding off on investing because I am nervous about timing the market or making a mistake. Help me understand the cost of staying on the sidelines. Show me how much more I would need to save each month if I delay investing by five or ten years compared to starting today."

Making Decisions with Discipline, Not Emotion
Addresses the Mistake: Letting Emotions Drive Decisions

- "Create a detailed, personalized checklist that will help me stay focused on my long-term investment goals, stick to my strategy, and avoid making trades based on short-term emotions or market noise."
- "Generate a plan for how I can respond calmly during market volatility, including specific steps to take and reminders to review to help me stay rational and aligned with my long-term goals."

Avoiding Big Bets and Staying Diversified
Addresses the Mistake: Overconcentration in One Stock or Sector

- "Analyze my portfolio for overweight positions in individual stocks, sectors, or asset classes, and recommend ways to diversify."
- "Look for overlapping holdings across my mutual funds or ETFs that may dilute diversification or add complexity."

Controlling What You Can: Costs and Efficiency
Addresses the Mistake: Ignoring Fees and Expenses

- "Compare my current portfolio's cost structure with a low-cost index fund alternative and estimate the impact over 10, 20, and 30 years."
- "Highlight any funds or positions with poor risk-adjusted returns relative to benchmarks and recommend cost-effective alternatives."

Avoiding the Trap of Chasing What Just Worked
Addresses the Mistake: Chasing Performance

- "Review my past investment decisions for signs of buying recent winners or selling recent losers and suggest a more disciplined approach."
- "Create a personalized set of rules or guardrails I can follow before making any new investment, such as evaluating long-term fundamentals and rechecking my asset allocation before acting on recent performance trends."

Keeping Your Portfolio in Balance
Addresses the Mistake: Not Rebalancing

- "Analyze my current portfolio and show how far each asset class has drifted from its target allocation. Also share recommendations for rebalancing to restore my desired mix."

- "Suggest strategies to rebalance in a tax-efficient manner using losses, asset location, or partial rebalancing."

Matching Your Portfolio to Your True Comfort with Risk
Addresses the Mistake: Misunderstanding Risk Tolerance

- "Compare my current portfolio's costs, performance, and diversification to a simple, low-cost three-fund portfolio to see if I am making things more complicated than they need to be."
- "Ask me a series of questions about my reactions to past market events and use the answers to recommend an asset mix that better fits my emotional comfort level."

Trading Less to Let Compounding Work
Addresses the Mistake: Overtrading

- "Review my portfolio to identify any tax-inefficient investments, such as bonds or REITs, held in taxable accounts, and recommend more tax-efficient asset locations for them."
- "Set up guidelines for when trading is justified, such as rebalancing, tax-loss harvesting, or a major life change, so that I can distinguish between thoughtful moves and trading unnecessarily."

Putting Time on Your Side
Addresses the Mistake: Not Investing at All

- "I'm nervous about investing because markets seem high right now. If I keep $10,000 in cash earning 4% instead of investing it in a diversified portfolio earning an assumed 8%, how much growth would I give up over 15 years?"

Staying Disciplined When It Matters Most

In the end, most investors are not defeated by market crashes but by their own reactions to them. Real success comes from staying invested, being consistent, and steering clear of costly mistakes. AI can help you do that. It can also spot what you might overlook, including blind spots, bias, or portfolio drift, and assess your decisions without emotion. With a steady second set of eyes, you can stay disciplined, focused, and better equipped to reach your goals.

CHAPTER 15

AVOIDING COMMON AI INVESTING MISTAKES

"Trust, but verify."
—Ronald Reagan

The biggest risks with AI in investing do not stem from the technology itself; they arise from how people use it. Overconfidence, poor prompts, or a lack of understanding can lead smart individuals to make costly mistakes. Therefore, if you want to use AI to support better financial decisions, you need to know where others go wrong and how to avoid those same pitfalls.

Mistake 1: Assuming the Output Is Always Right
One of the easiest mistakes to make is believing that because AI responds with confidence, it must be correct. That is not how it works. AI is trained on large volumes of text and data. Some of that content is outdated, and some reflects a specific bias or investment philosophy that may not match your own.

For example, if you ask AI, "What is the best ETF for commodities investing?" it will try to provide a clear answer. But what does "best" mean in this context? Highest return over the past year? Lowest fees? Most assets under management? Best risk-adjusted performance? You may receive a real fund name in response, but the result depends entirely on how the model interprets your question.

That is why it is essential to verify any investment recommendation. Look up the fund, check the holdings, and compare it to your goals and risk tolerance. AI can suggest a starting point, but it cannot confirm whether something is right for you. You must do that part.

Ways to check AI output:

- Cross-Check with Reliable Sources: Look up tickers, fund statistics, or strategies on trusted sites like Morningstar, Yahoo Finance, or the fund provider's page.

- Ask Follow-Up Questions: Challenge the output: "What are the risks?" or "Why is this a good fit for my goals?"

- Compare with Other Tools: Run the same query on multiple platforms to see if results are consistent.

- Use Common Sense: Ask yourself, "Does this make sense based on my risk tolerance, time horizon, and financial plan?"

- Use Common Benchmarks: Compare recommendations to simple, low-cost ETFs to see if the suggestion adds value.

- Watch for Confident Nonsense: If the output includes bold claims with no citations, double-check. AI can sound right and still occasionally be wrong.

- Get a Second Opinion: Run the same prompt in a different AI program to compare results, ask a professional, or plug the output into a spreadsheet.[67] At a minimum, ask AI to

---

67   If you want to see how reliable your AI output really is, try running the same prompt in a different AI program and compare the results.

reveal its work and assumptions. Seeing how different tools respond can help you spot inconsistencies.

Mistake 2: Not Giving Enough Context

AI tools can only respond based on what you provide. If your prompt is vague, the answer will be vague, and if your prompt is generic, the answer will be generic. That may seem obvious, but many people type short, open-ended questions like, "How should I invest?" or "What is the right portfolio for me?" without including the details that actually matter. The better your input, the better your output. A more effective prompt might be something like the following:

"I am 38 years old, married with two kids, currently maxing out my Roth IRA and 401(k). I have $50,000 in savings, a moderate risk tolerance, and I hope to retire around age 60. What is a sensible asset allocation for my situation, and which ETFs or mutual funds align with that?"

This prompt gives AI something substantial to work with. It narrows the scope, defines the constraints, and makes the response more relevant. You still need to review the output critically, but at least it is grounded in your situation and provides a good starting point.

Tools like Claude, Gemini, or Perplexity can give you slightly different perspectives, and, in some cases, you might even check with something more specialized like Wolfram Alpha for calculations. For example, if you ask about the benefits of diversification, one AI tool might give you a textbook explanation while another highlights practical, real-world examples, and a calculation tool could show you the math behind portfolio risk. Putting those pieces together offers you a fuller, more trustworthy answer.

Mistake 3: Using AI to Chase Hot Stocks

Some investors use AI as a new way to try to find the next big stock. They ask for trending stocks, look for short-term winners, or try to find the next big thing. It is tempting because AI can scan social media, news headlines, and earnings reports faster than any human ever could. However, just because a stock is trending does not mean it is a good investment. Momentum is not a substitute for fundamentals, and popularity does not equal long-term value. If you are using AI to make quick trades without understanding the business, the risks, or how that decision fits into your overall plan, then you are not really investing; you are speculating.

You can ask AI to explain what a company does, summarize risks, compare competitors, or translate financial terminology without technical jargon. This is where AI can really help. However, if you rely on it to tell you what to buy next based solely on forums or recent returns, then you are setting yourself up for disappointment.

Mistake 4: Not Protecting Your Financial Data

Another area where investors need to be careful is data privacy. Using AI to explore your finances does not mean giving up your privacy, but you need to be intentional about what you share and how you use the tool.

A few simple guidelines can help:

- Do not share sensitive information like your Social Security number, account numbers, or home address.
- When describing your financial situation, use round numbers or estimates unless you are working in a secure environment.

- Ask the platform, "Do you store my data or use it to train future models?"
- Give preference to platforms that offer encryption, clear privacy policies, and the option to delete or anonymize your inputs.

AI Is a Tool, Not a Shortcut

AI can make you a better investor by giving you clearer information and insights. It can compare options, highlight risks, and organize your thinking. What it cannot do, however, is make the decisions for you. Think of AI as an assistant that helps you prepare, not as a substitute for doing the work. The real progress comes when you use AI to learn more, ask better questions, and test your assumptions. Used this way, it keeps you engaged, avoids the mistakes that set many investors back, and helps you stick to your plan.

FINAL THOUGHTS

You made it! You reached the end of this journey, and I hope you feel proud of the progress you have made. You have worked through the prompts and planning steps that can help you see your financial life with more clarity and purpose. You now have a stronger understanding of what you want to achieve and how to create an investment strategy that fits your goals and values.

Throughout these pages, my goal was never to hand you a formula or promise a perfect system. Instead, I wanted to demonstrate to you how to think, question, and use AI as a practical tool to strengthen your decision-making. I wanted to help you use technology to support your goals, not replace your judgment.

By now, you understand that investing well is not about trying to guess what comes next but about making choices that fit your priorities and managing risk in a way that feels right for you. It also means staying consistent through different market conditions. You have learned how to use AI to explore possibilities, test your thinking, and identify areas you might have missed. You also know that you do not need to have all the answers before you begin. What matters most is that you take the first step and keep learning along the way.

If you are just starting, begin with small, consistent steps: open the account, then make your first contribution, then check your assumptions, and then use AI to help you think through options and stay organized. Progress builds through motion, not perfection.

If you are already investing, this same mindset applies. Use AI to review your portfolio, reflect on your goals, and consider adjustments as your life evolves. Sometimes, the most valuable thing AI can do is help you slow down and think before you make a change.

As you move forward, remember that financial success is not only about numbers. It is also about understanding yourself. You will learn what kind of volatility you can tolerate, what trade-offs you are willing to make, and what peace of mind looks like for you. That awareness will guide you far more effectively than any model or algorithm.

Use AI when it helps you learn or saves you time, but keep your judgment at the center. The combination of your insight and the tools available to you today can be powerful when used thoughtfully. My hope is that this book leaves you feeling ready to put what you have learned into action.

The future you want begins with the choices you make today. Start where you are, use what you have, and move forward with purpose.